Clarence Robert Tower

A COLLECTION OF PAINTINGS AND DRAWINGS –

CITY OF SANTA CLARA & CENTRAL CALIFORNIA

COPYRIGHT

San Francisco

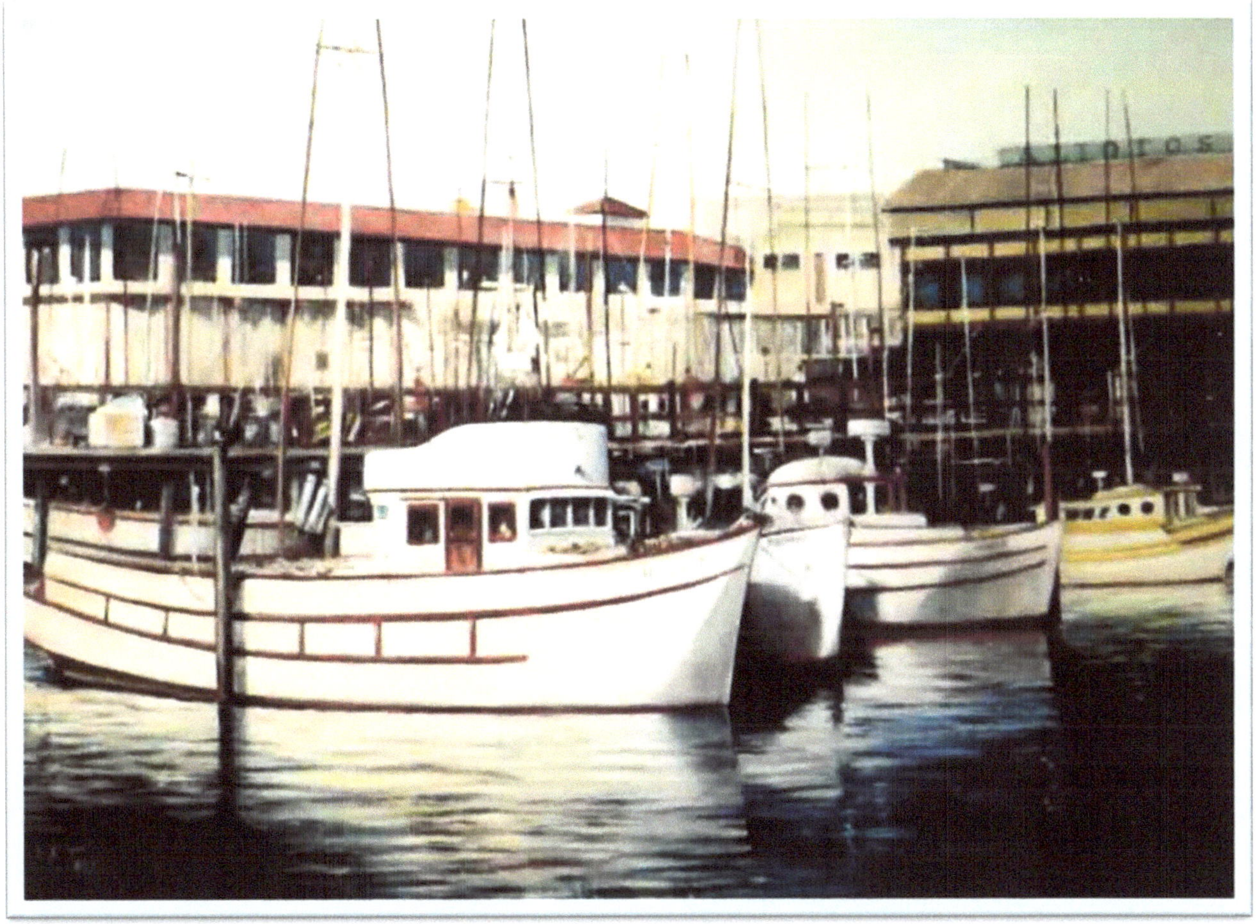

Fisherman's Wharf

A San Jose Landmark

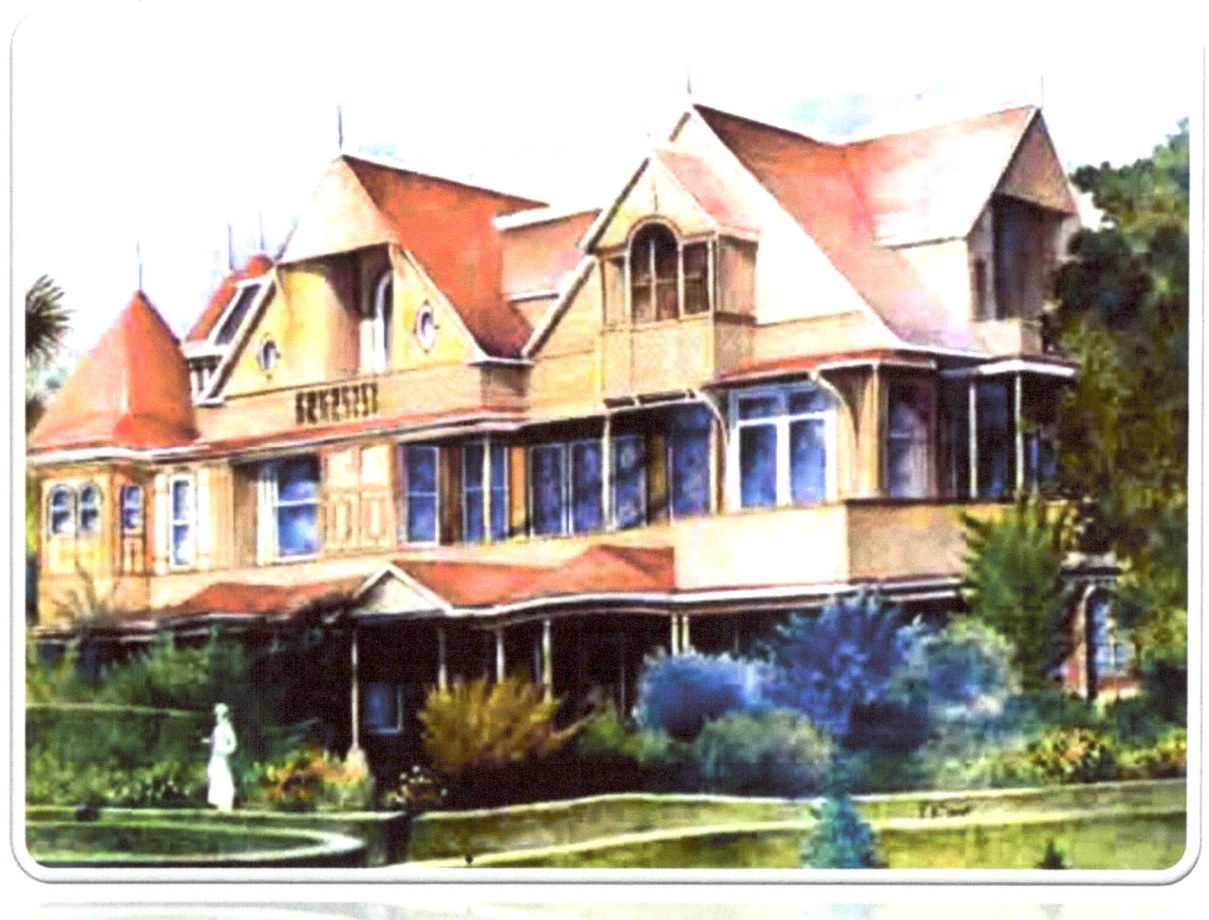

Winchester Mystery House
525 S. Winchester Blvd.

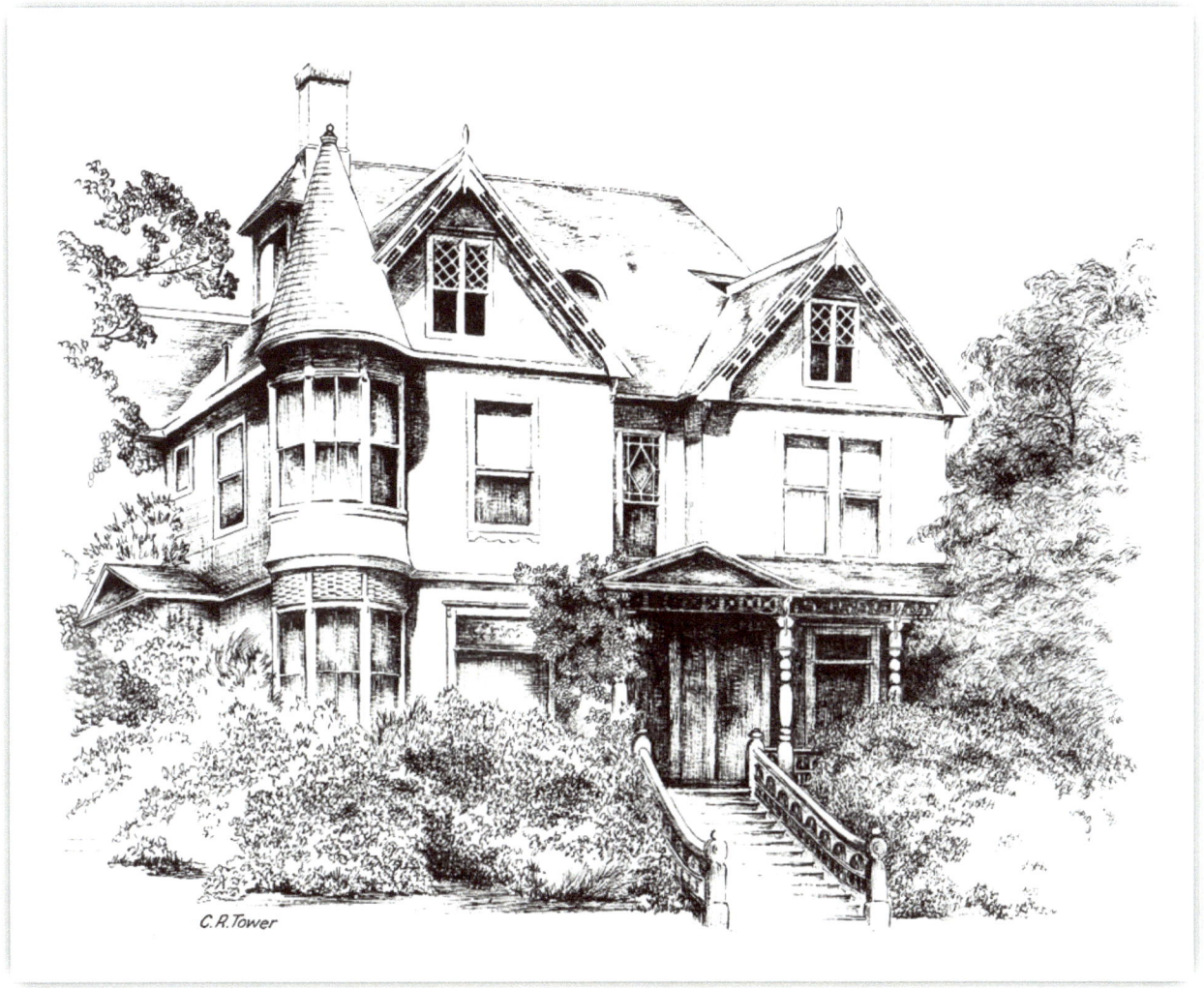

**Charles Copland Morse Mansion,
Founder of Ferry–Morse Seed Company
981 Fremont Street**

City of Santa Clara Images

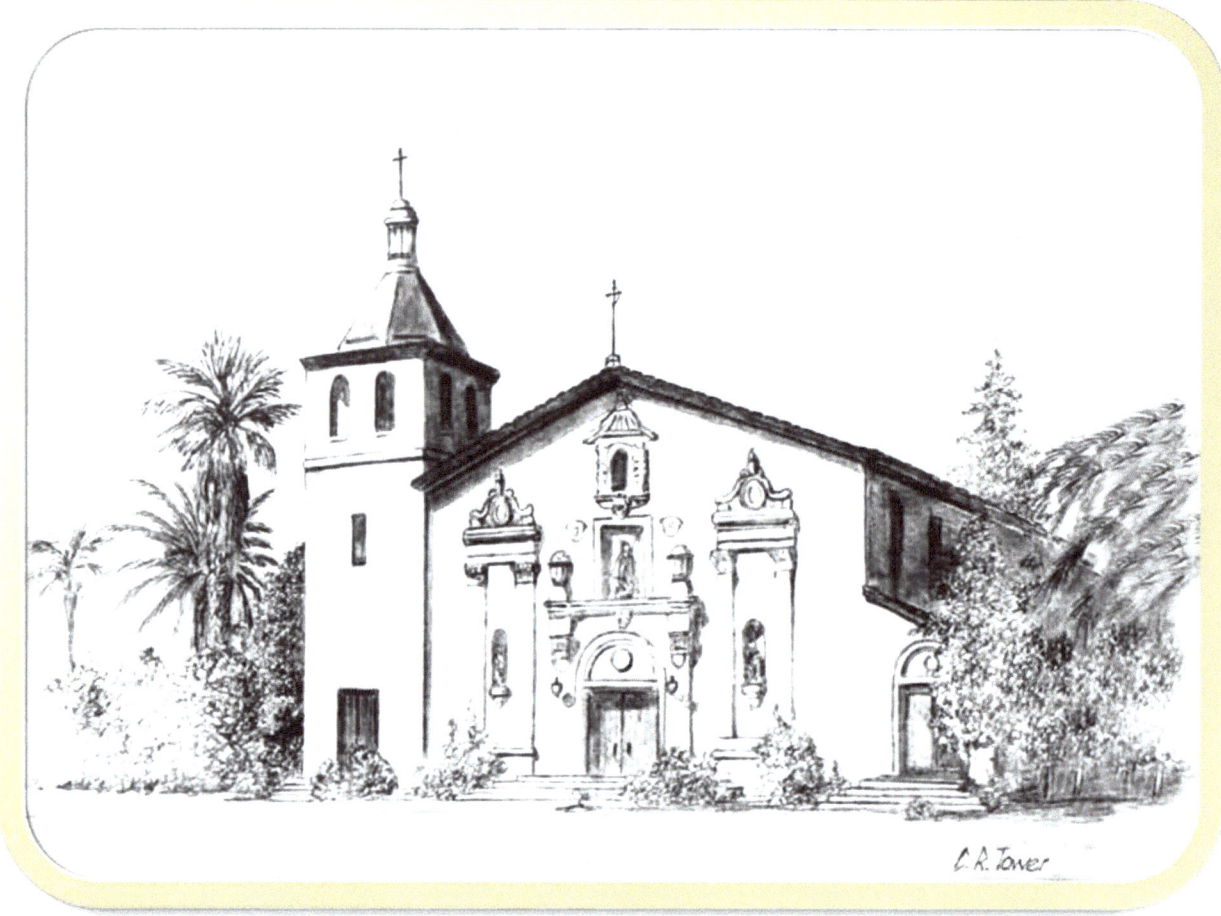

Mission Santa Clara
Located on grounds of Santa Clara University.

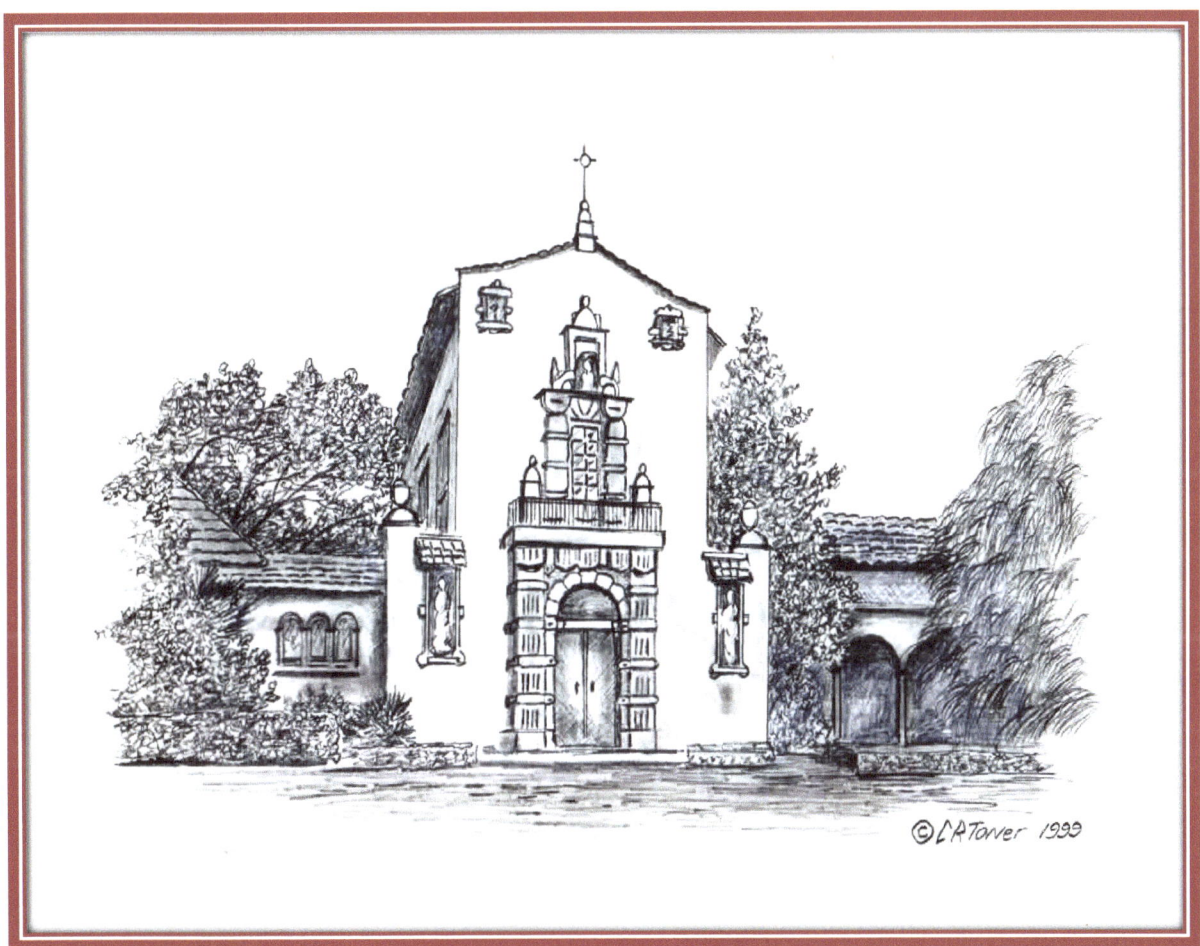

Carmelite Monastery
1000 Lincoln Street

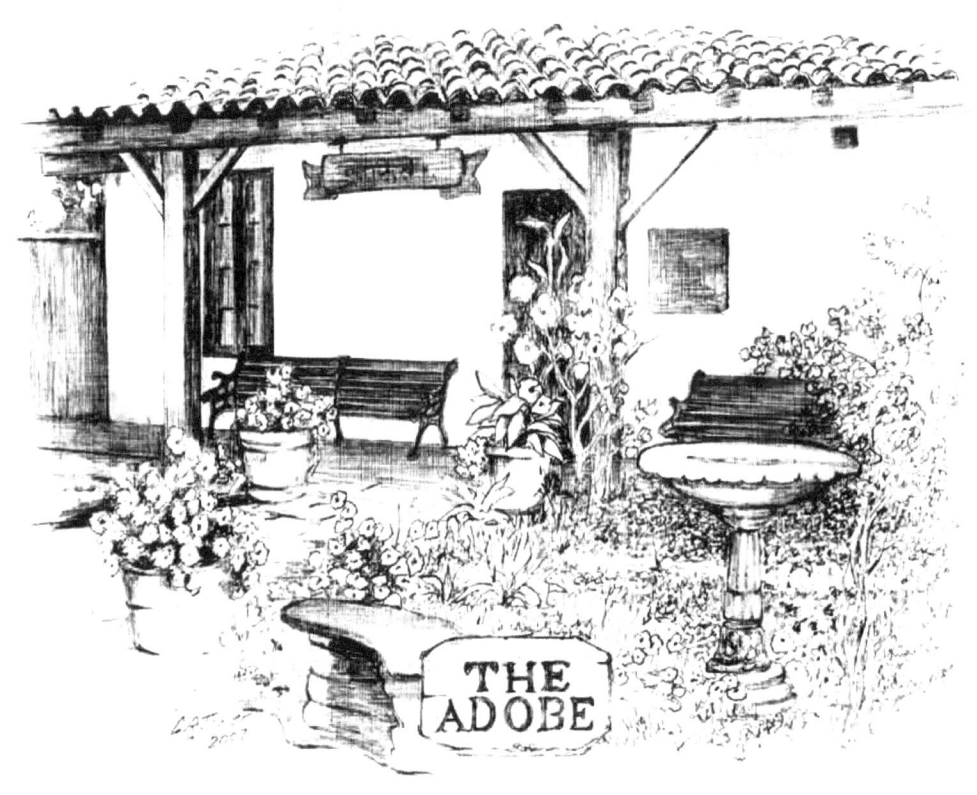

Santa Clara Women's Club Adobe
3260 The Alameda
(Old El Camino Real)
A short distance north of original Santa Clara University grounds.

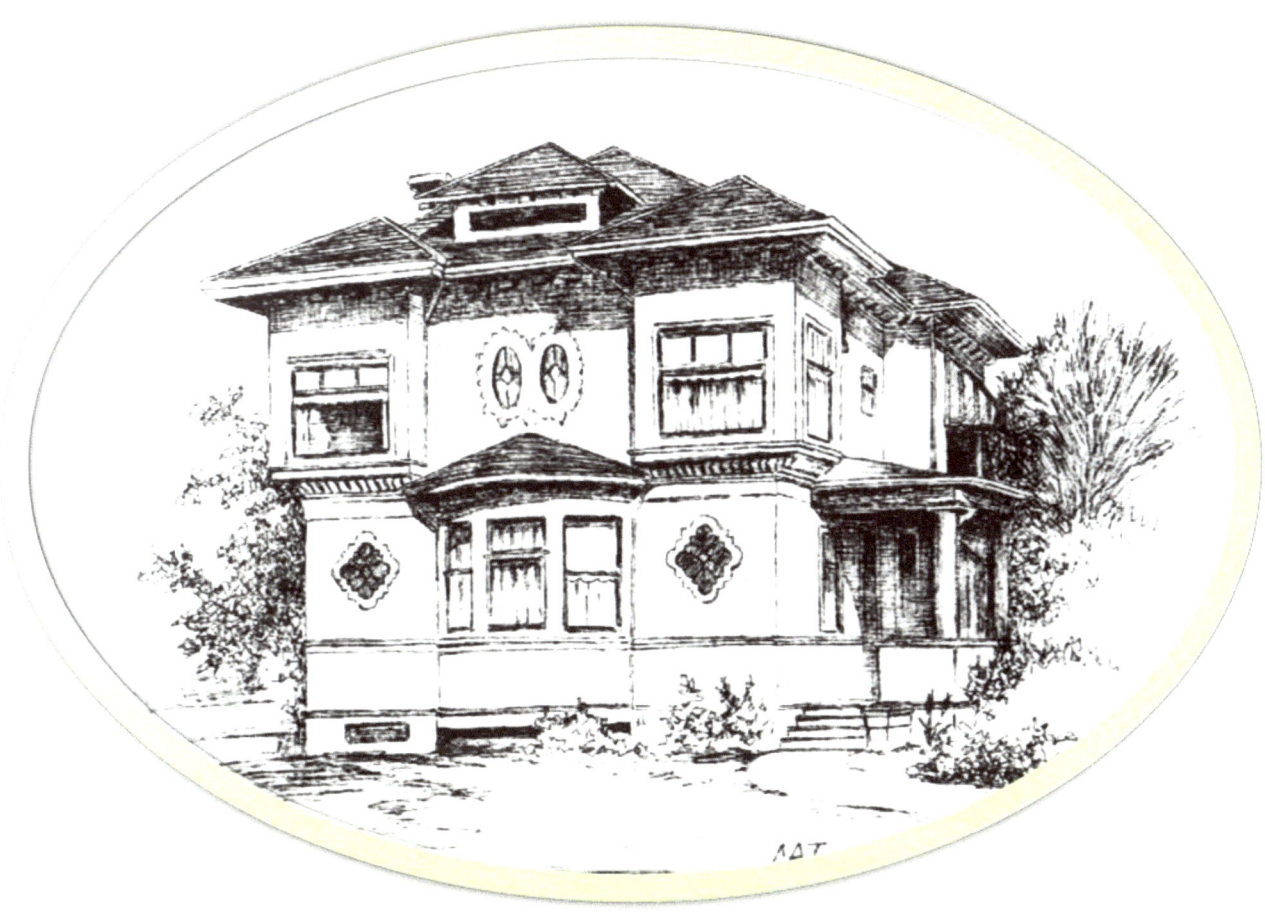

F. C. Franck II, Mansion
1179 Washington Street

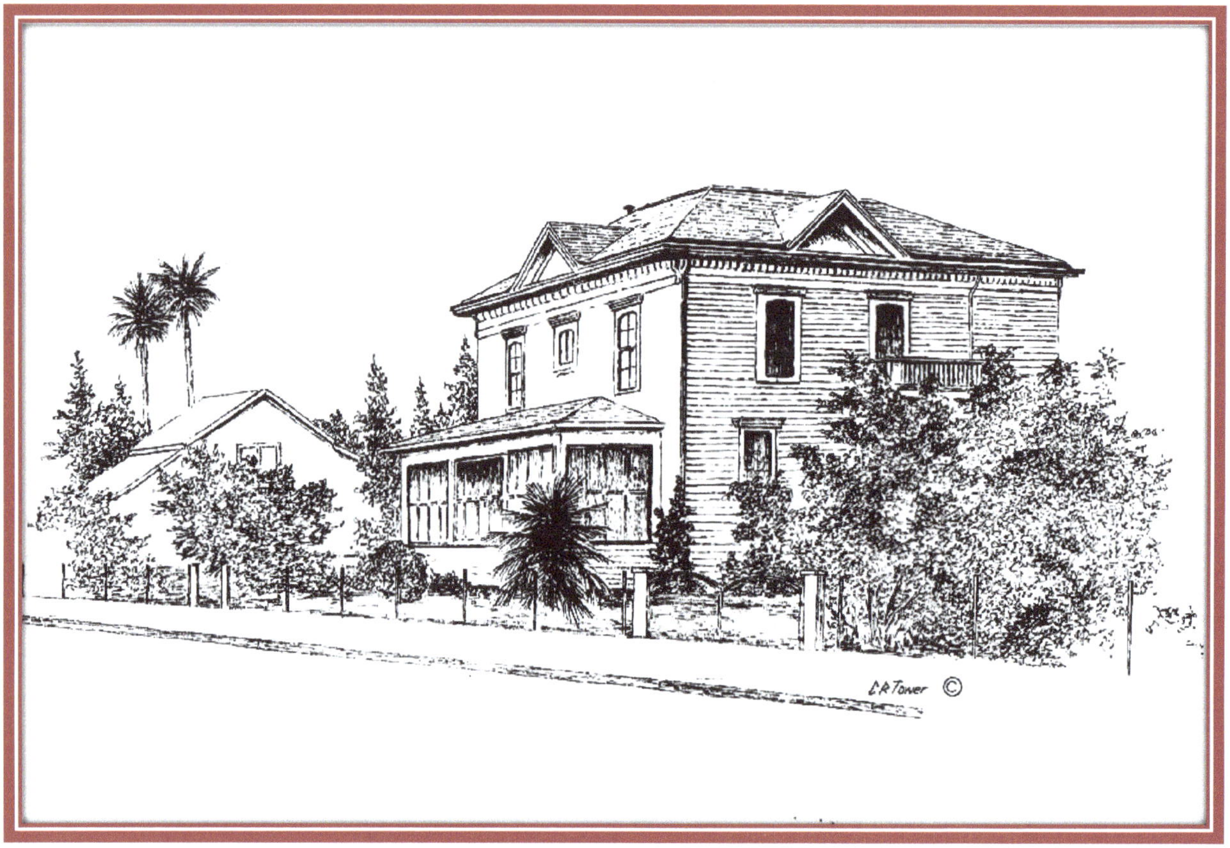

Harris-Lass Museum
1889 Market Street

City of Santa Clara Images

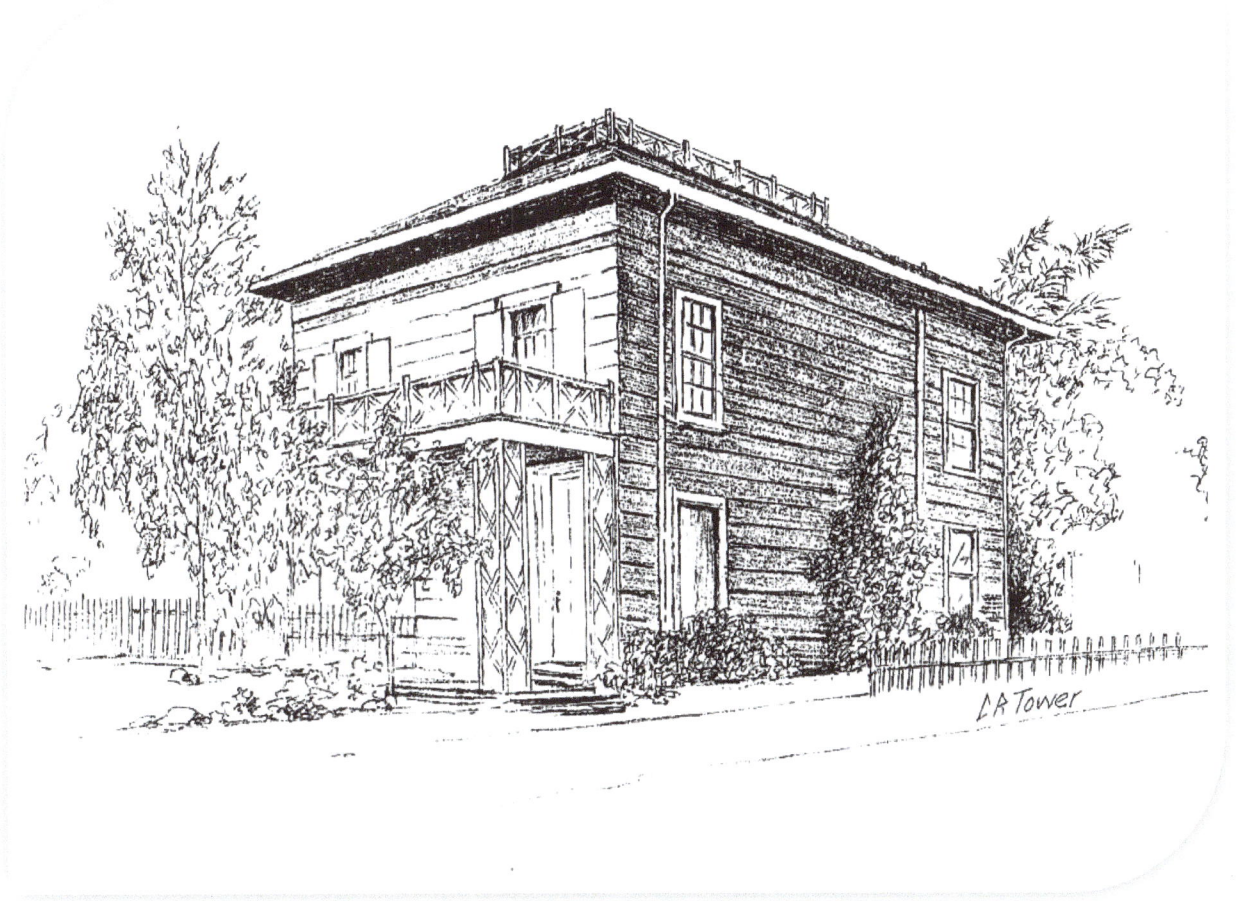

Johnson House
1159 Main Street

City of Santa Clara Images

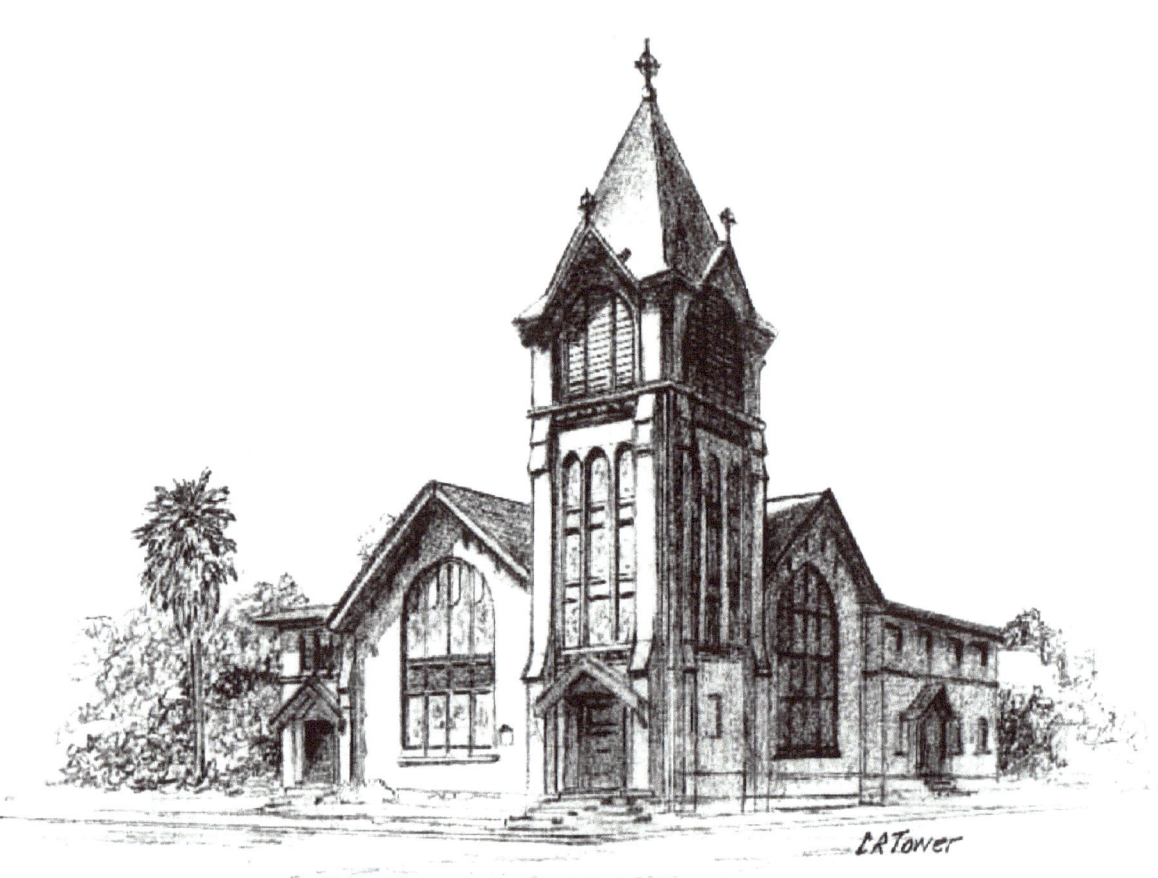

Old First Christian Church
Homestead Road at Main Street
(No longer standing)

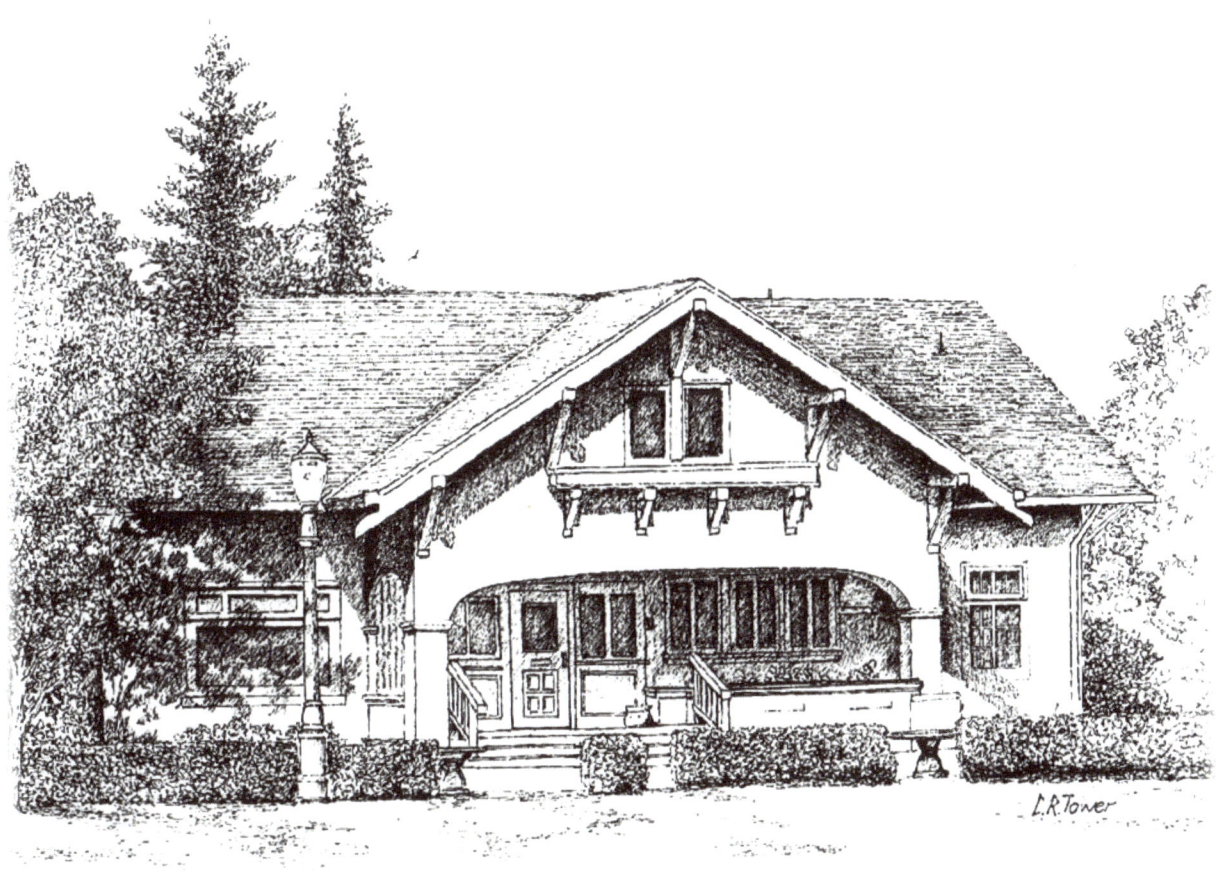

Headen-Inman House
On grounds of Triton Museum of Art – Warburton Avenue

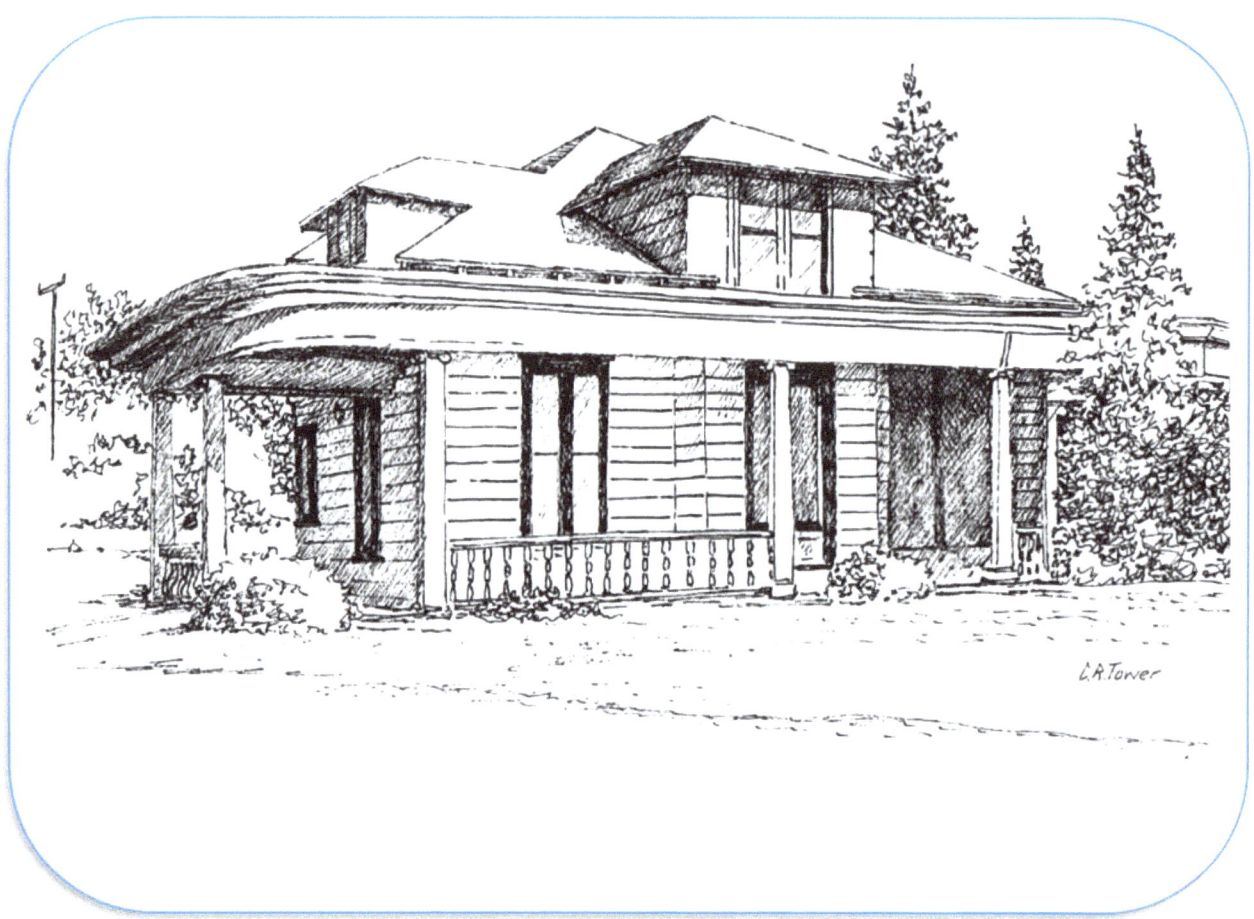

Jamison – Brown House
On grounds of Triton Museum of Art - Warburton Avenue

City of Santa Clara Images

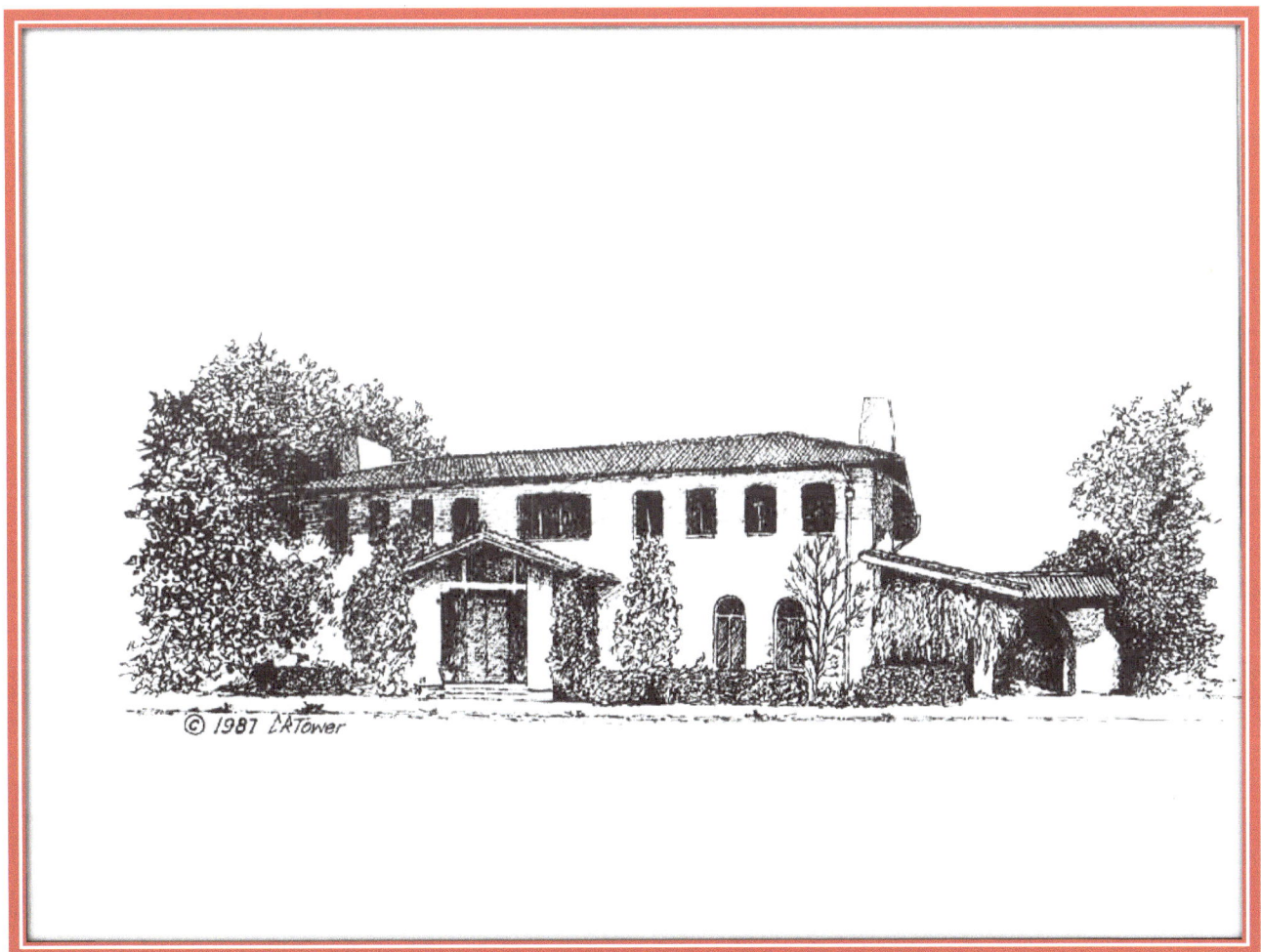

Former Agnew State Hospital Headquarters
(This is the first in a following list of homes and structures featured during Santa Clara's Annual Christmas Home Tours)

City of Santa Clara Images

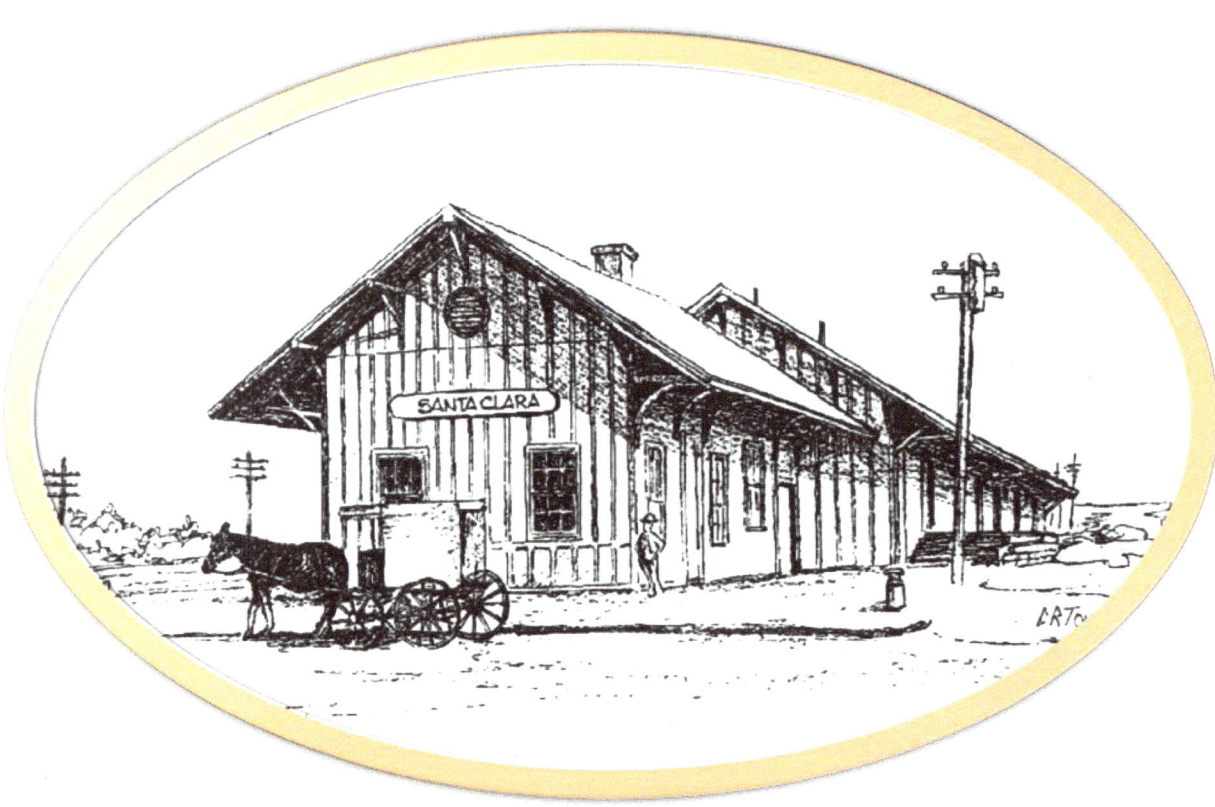

Santa Clara Railroad Station – 1065 Railroad Avenue
(Currently a Railroad Museum and Model Railroad Display
Also a Christmas Home Tour Contributor)

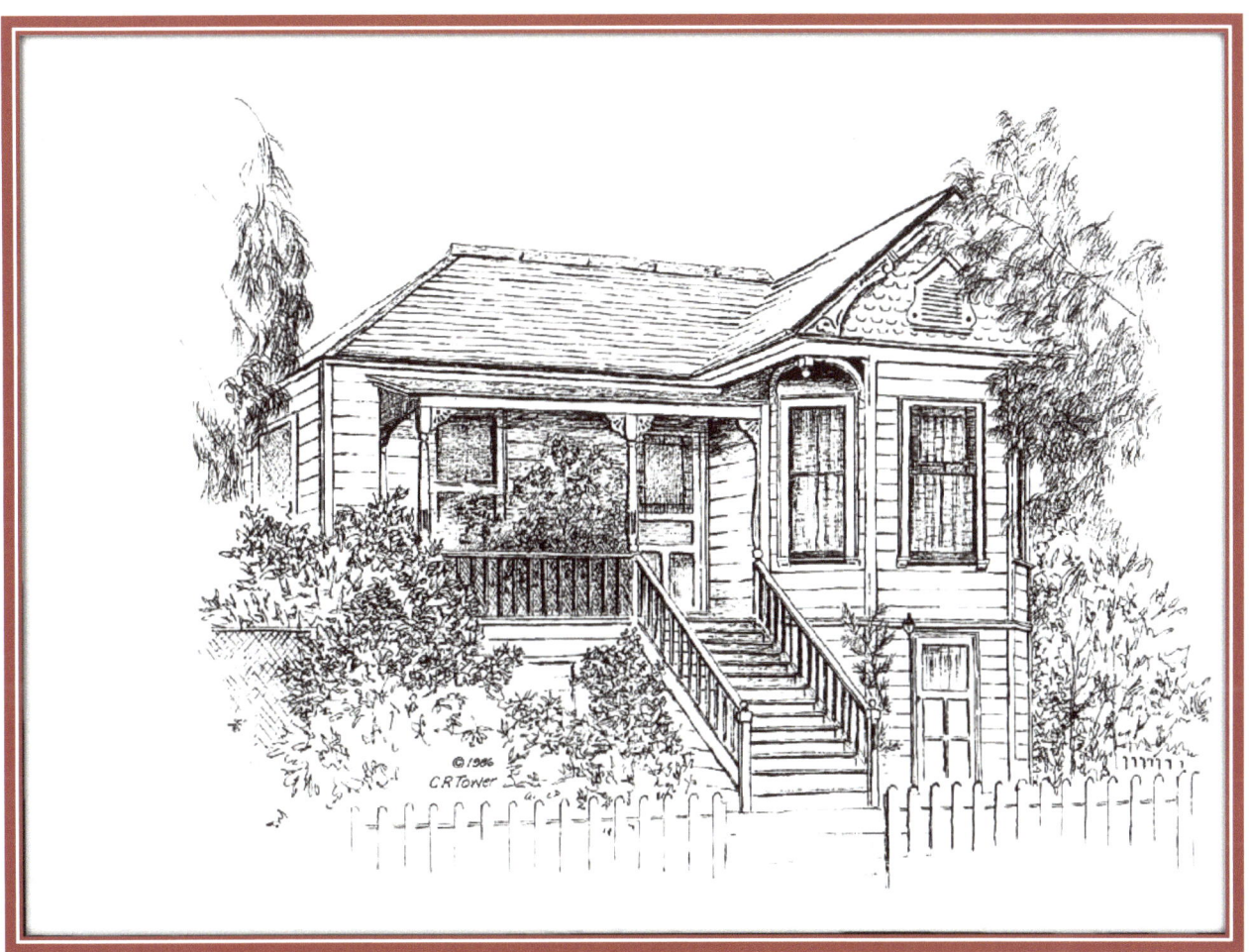

Madison Street Inn – 1390 Madison Street
(Home Tour Contributor)

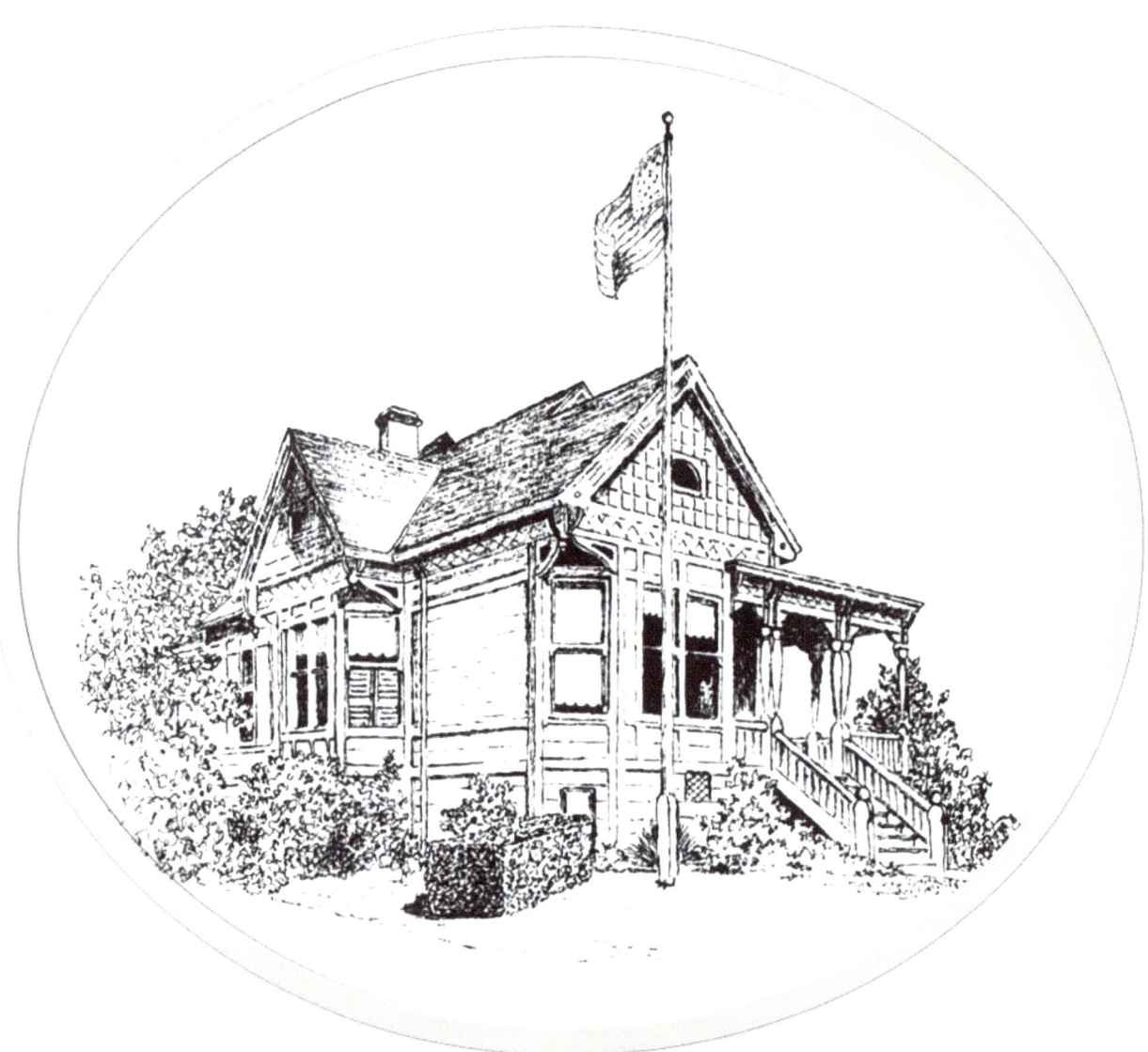

Palmer House – 1195 Main Street
(Home Tour Contributor)

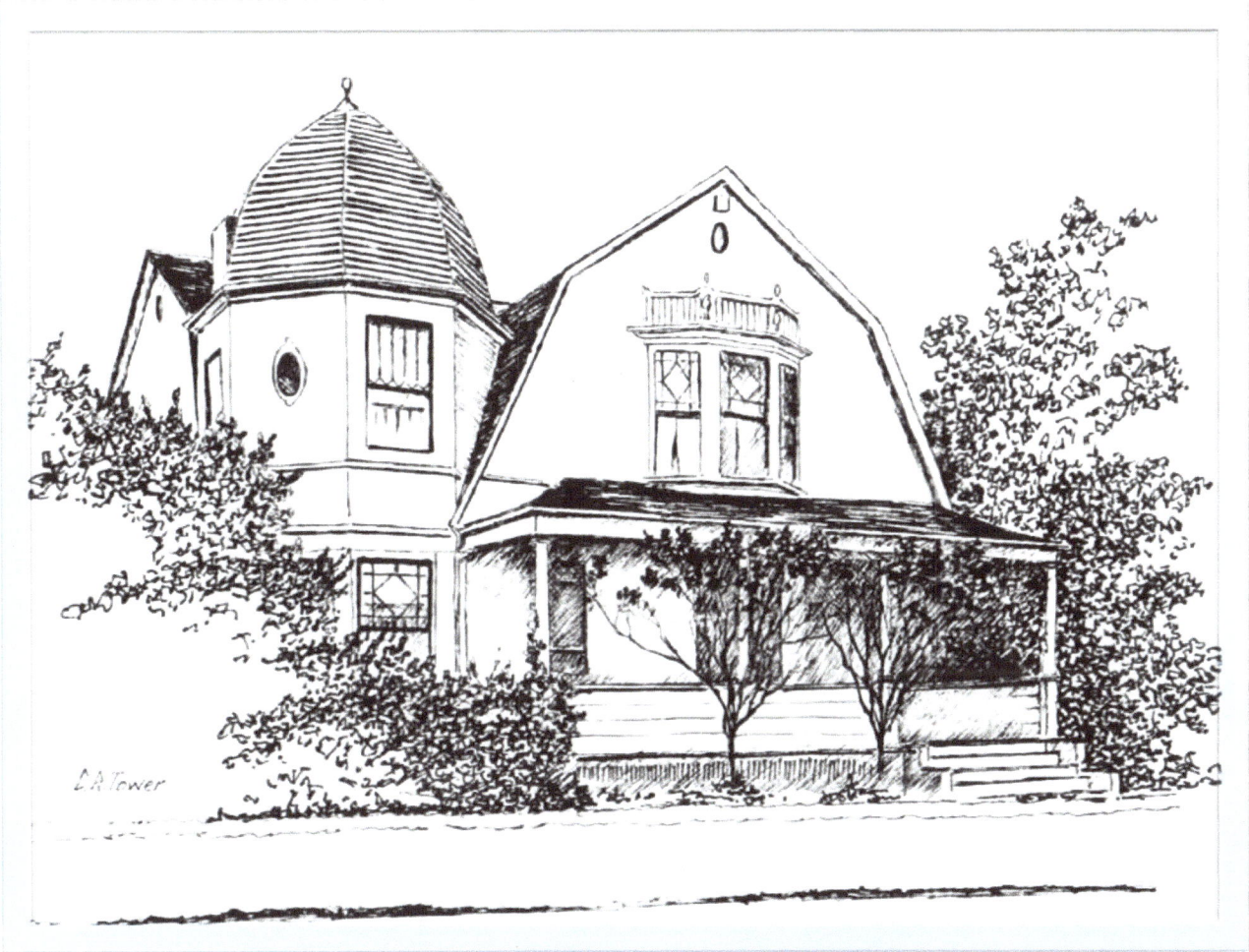

1893 Queen Anne – 610 Monroe Street
(Home Tour Contributor)

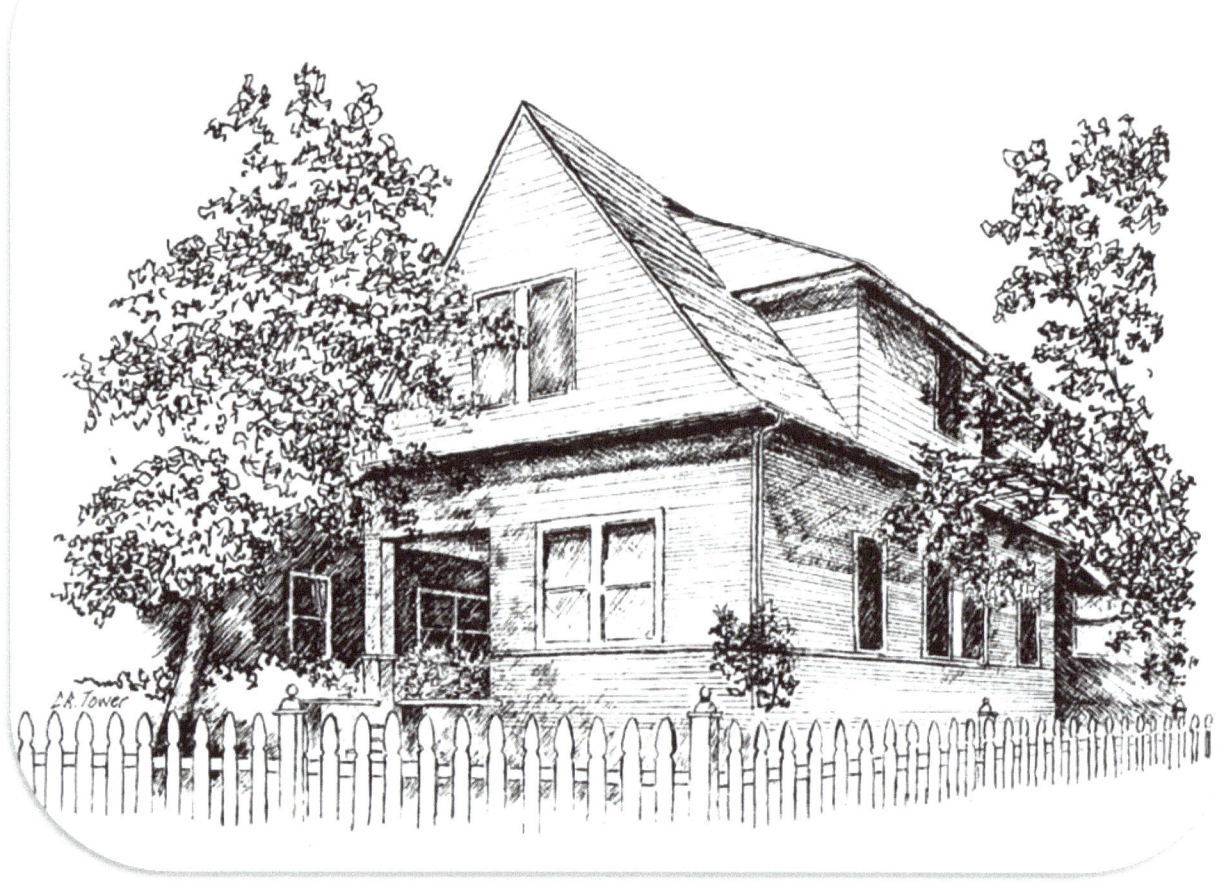

1900s Shingle – 811 Monroe Street
(Home Tour contributor)

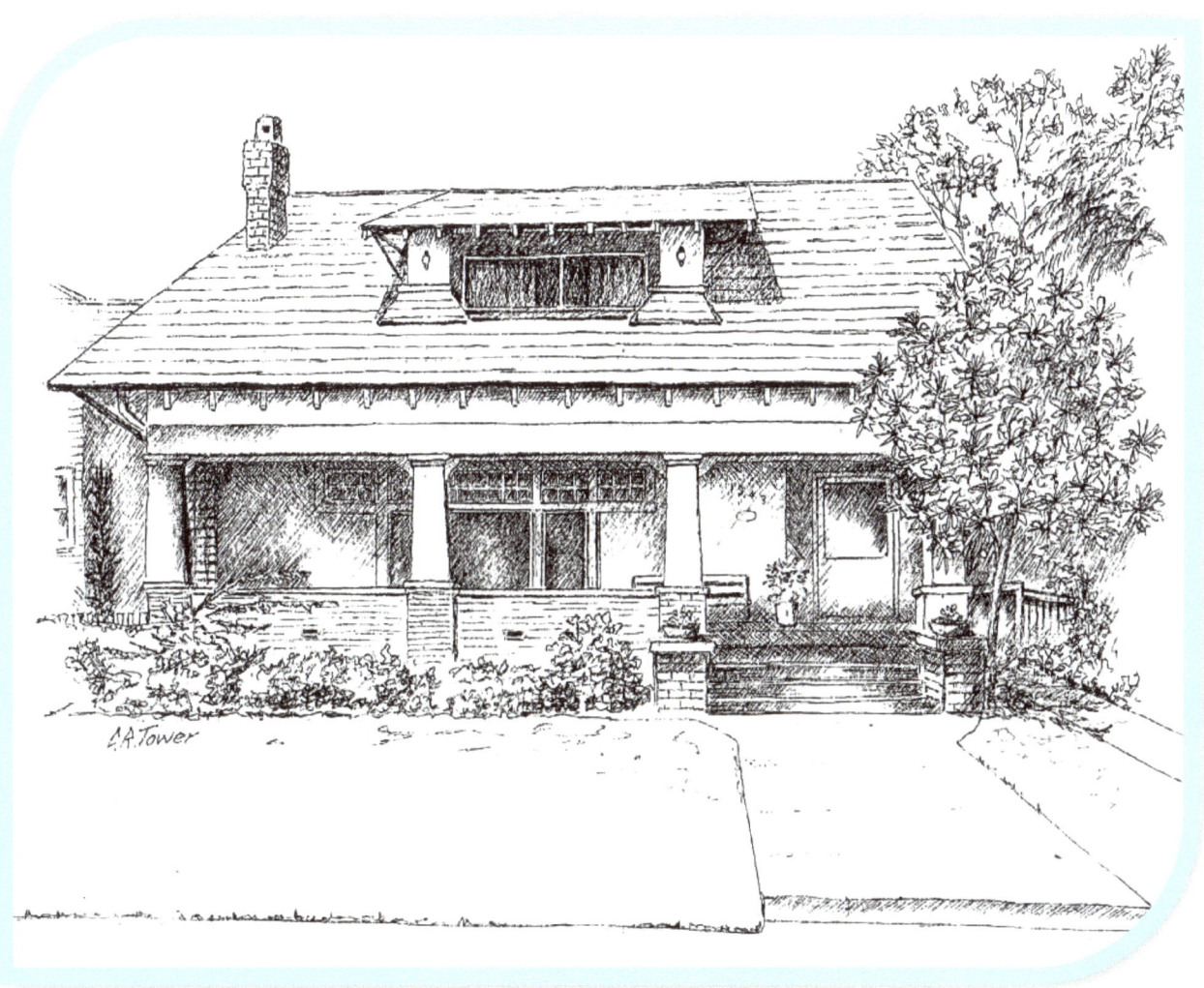

Semas House - 1543 Franklin Street
(Home Tour Contributor)

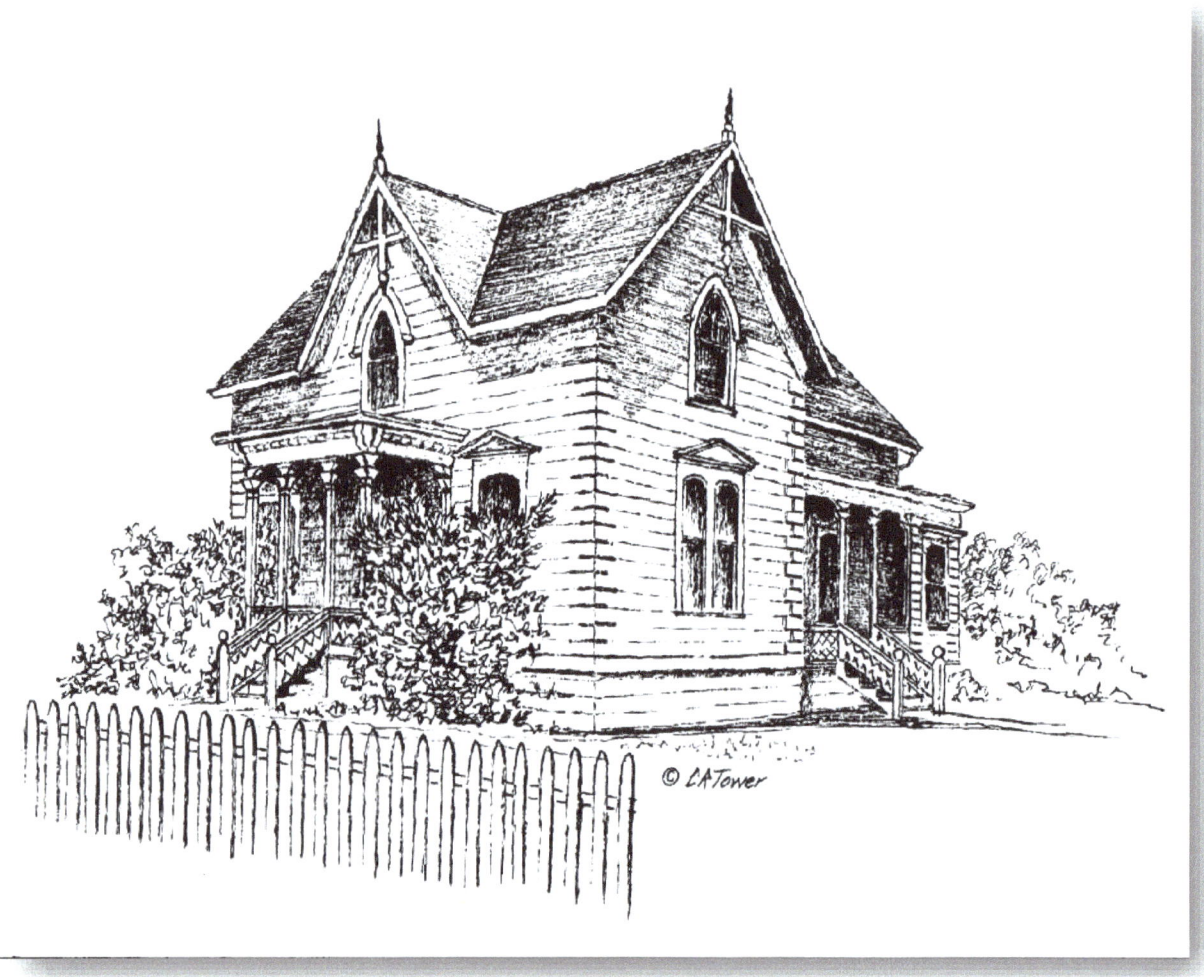

Landrum House – 1217 Santa Clara Street
(Home Tour Contributor)

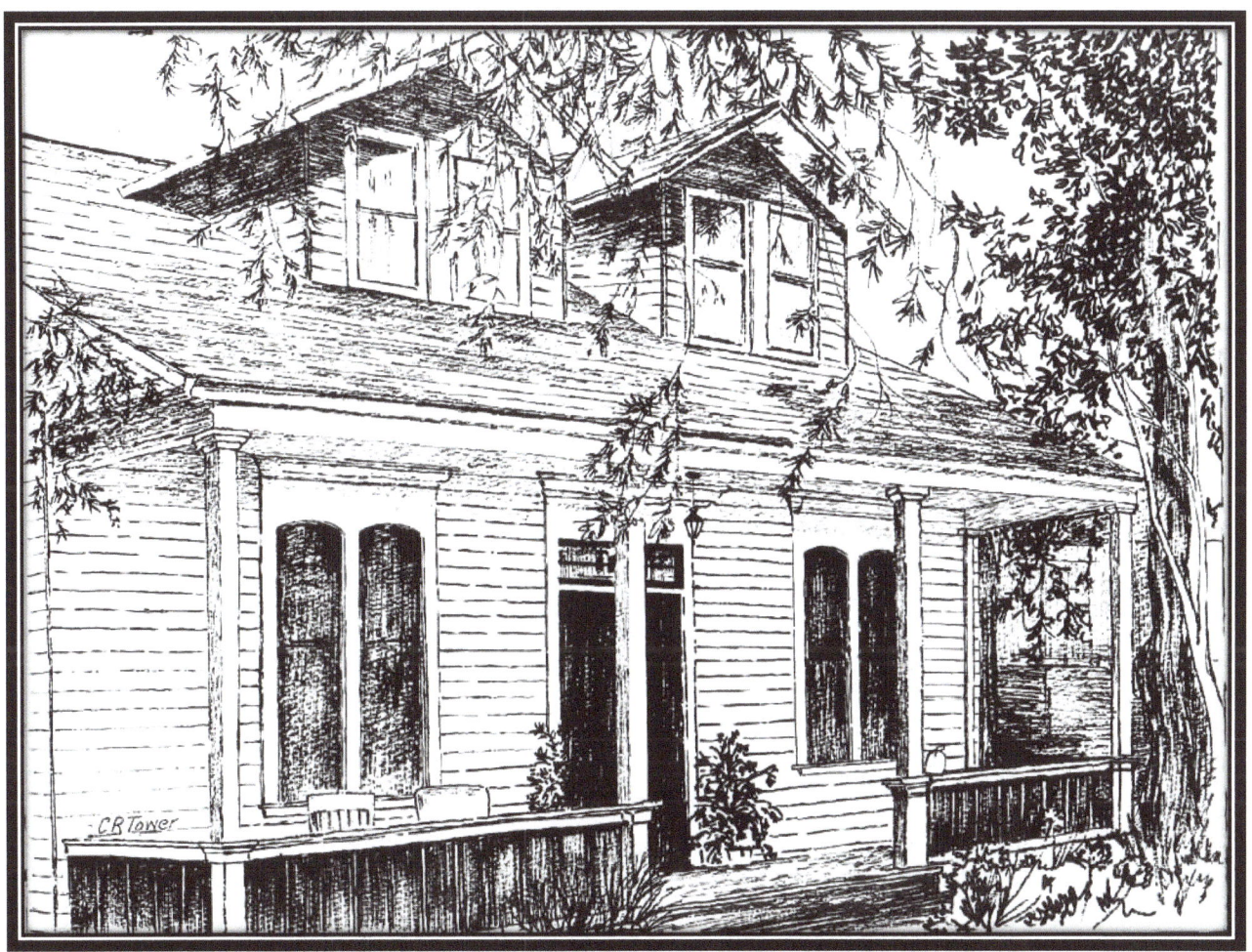

Peebles – Hichborn House – 1091 Fremont Street
(Two-time Home Tour Contributor)

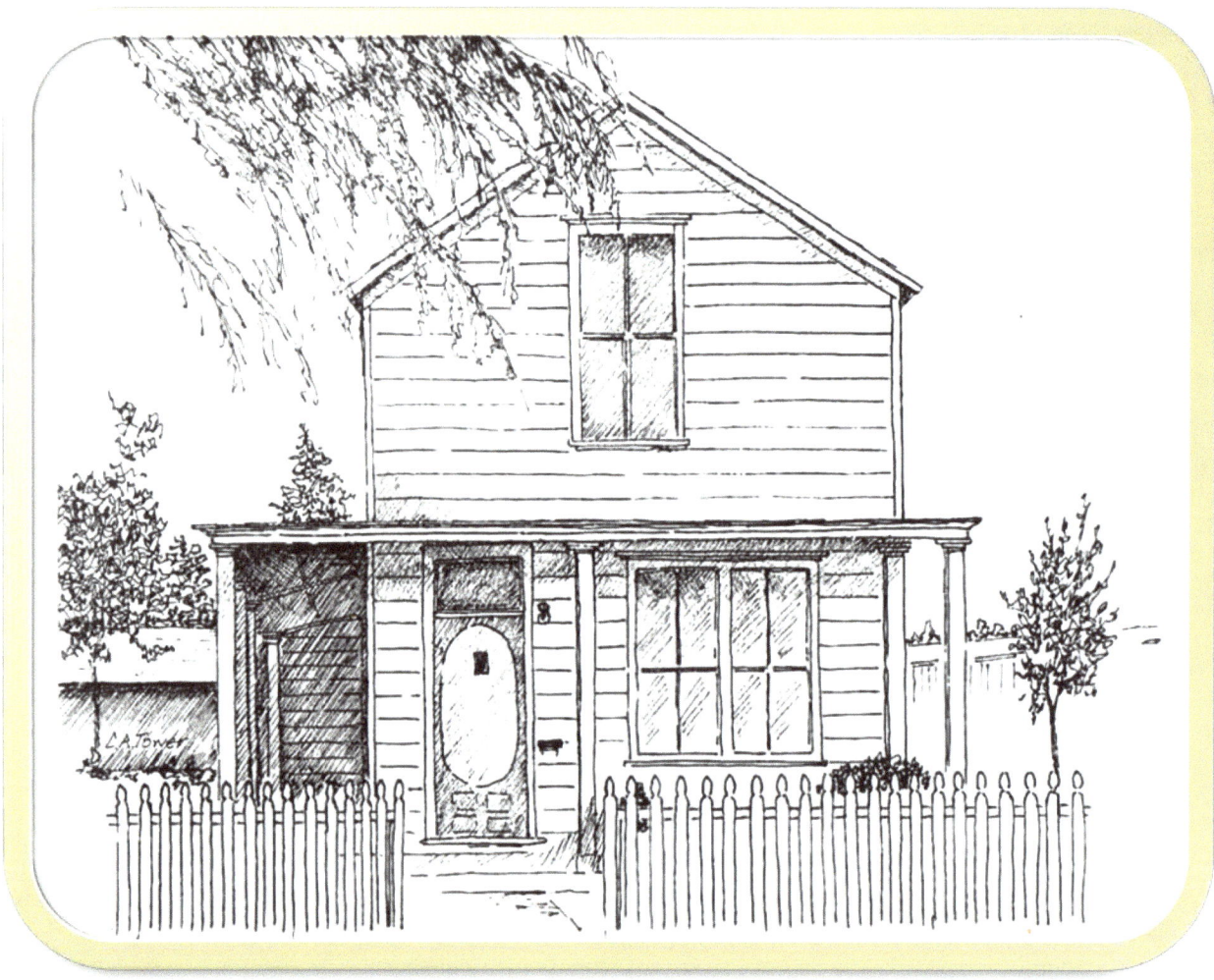

1880s Greek revival - 1404 Lincoln Street
(Home Tour Contributor)

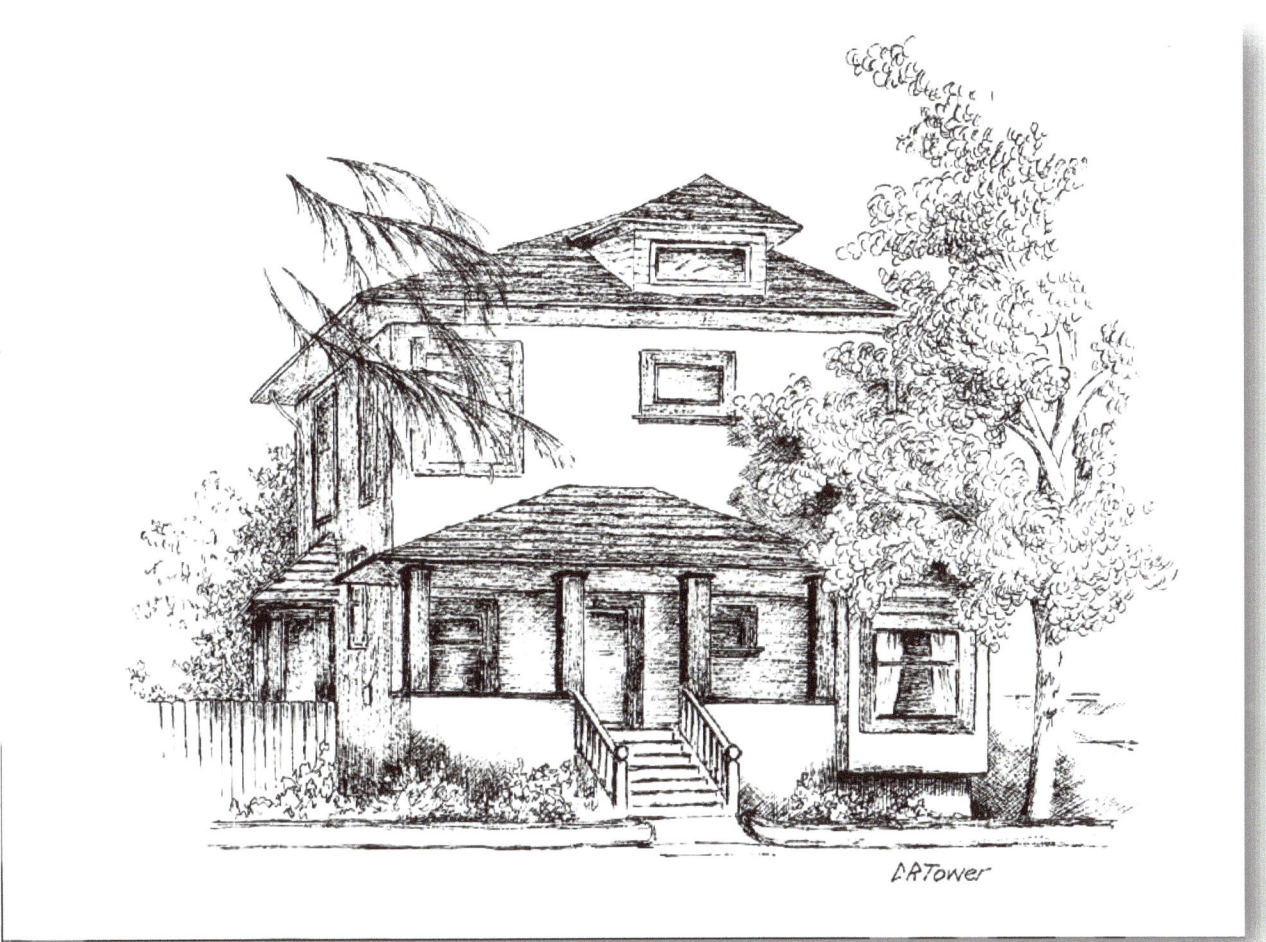

McIntyre House - 1540 Homestead Road
(Home Tour Contributor)

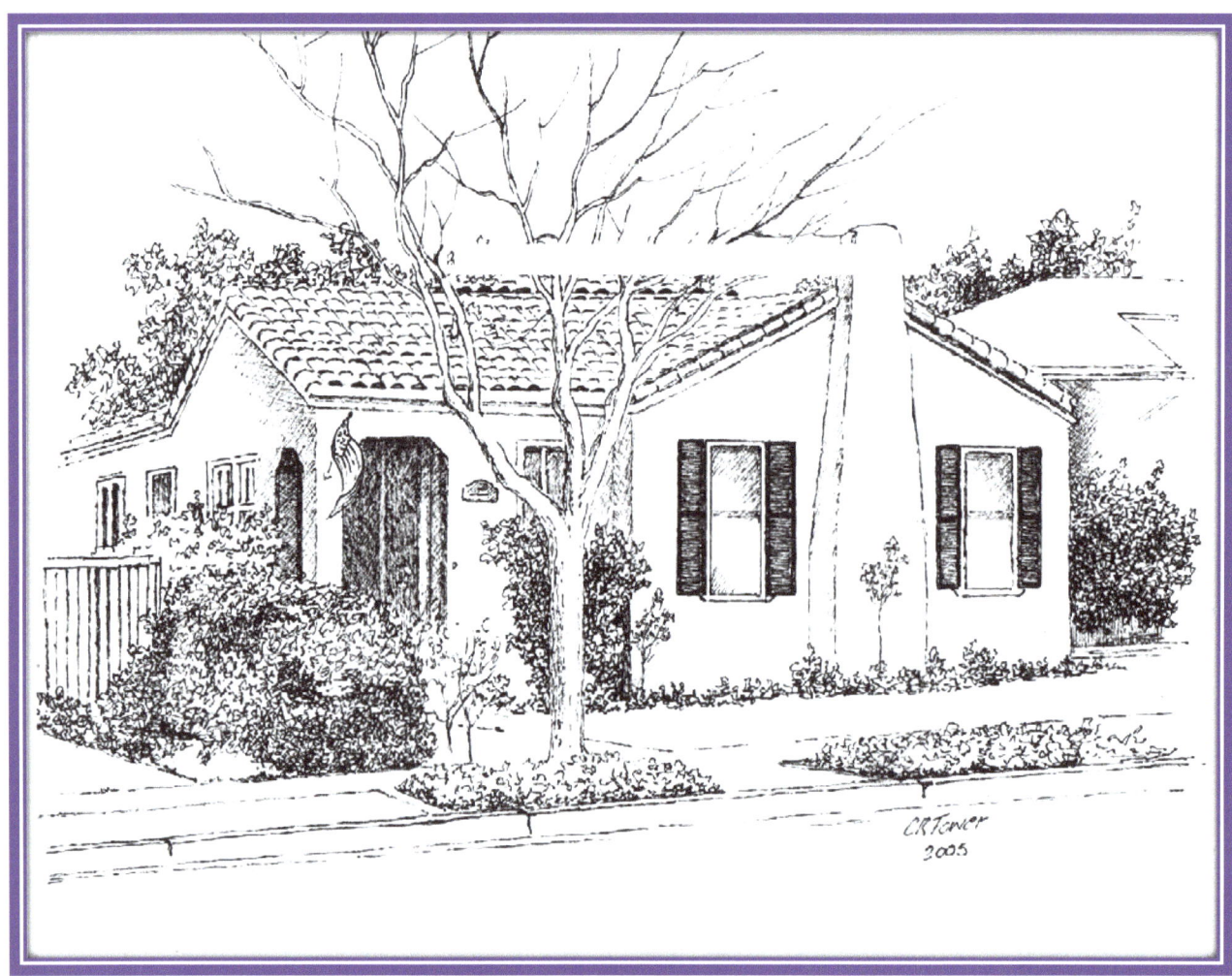

Caserta – South House
936 Fremont Street

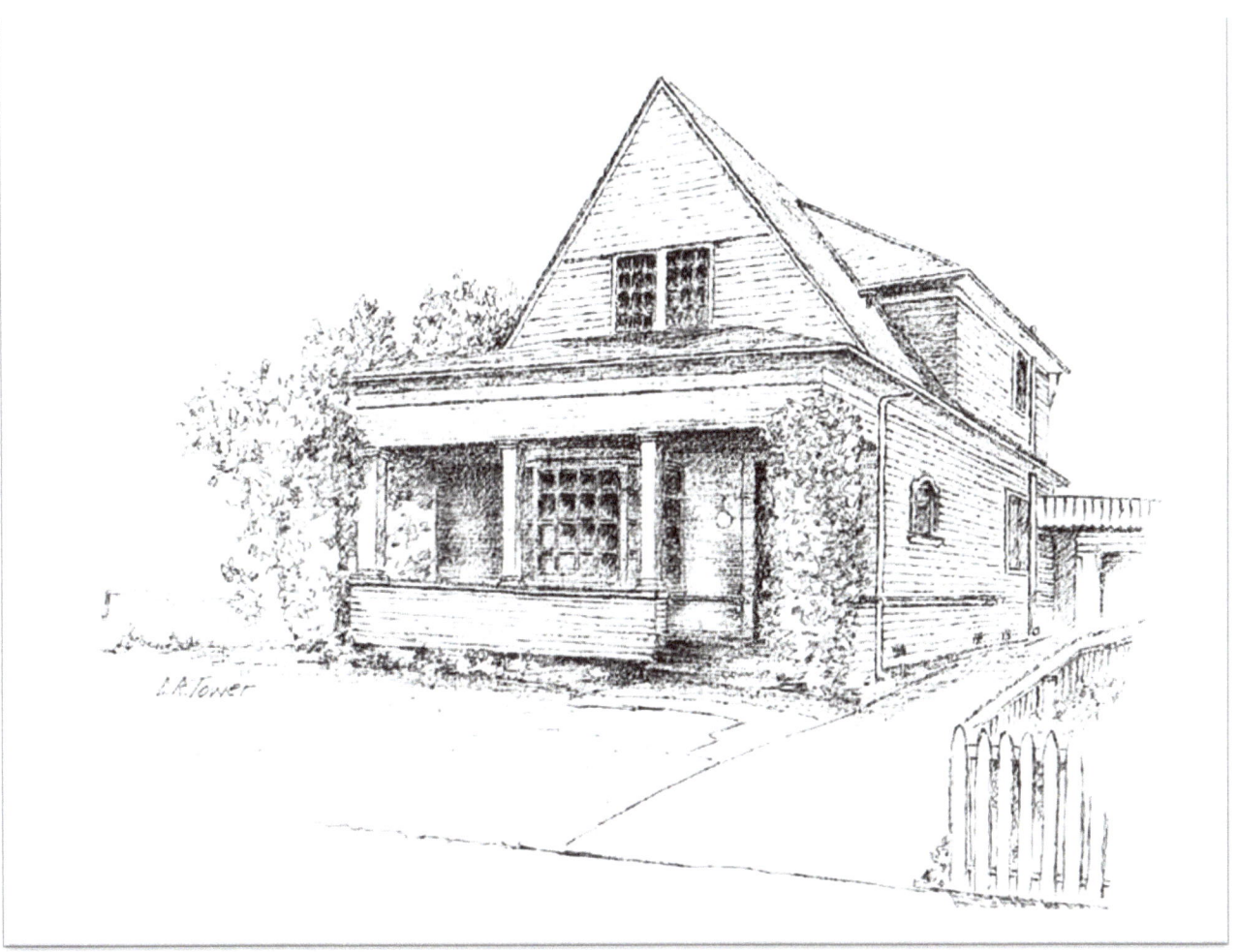

Baptist Church Parsonage - 864 Madison Street
(Home Tour Contributor)

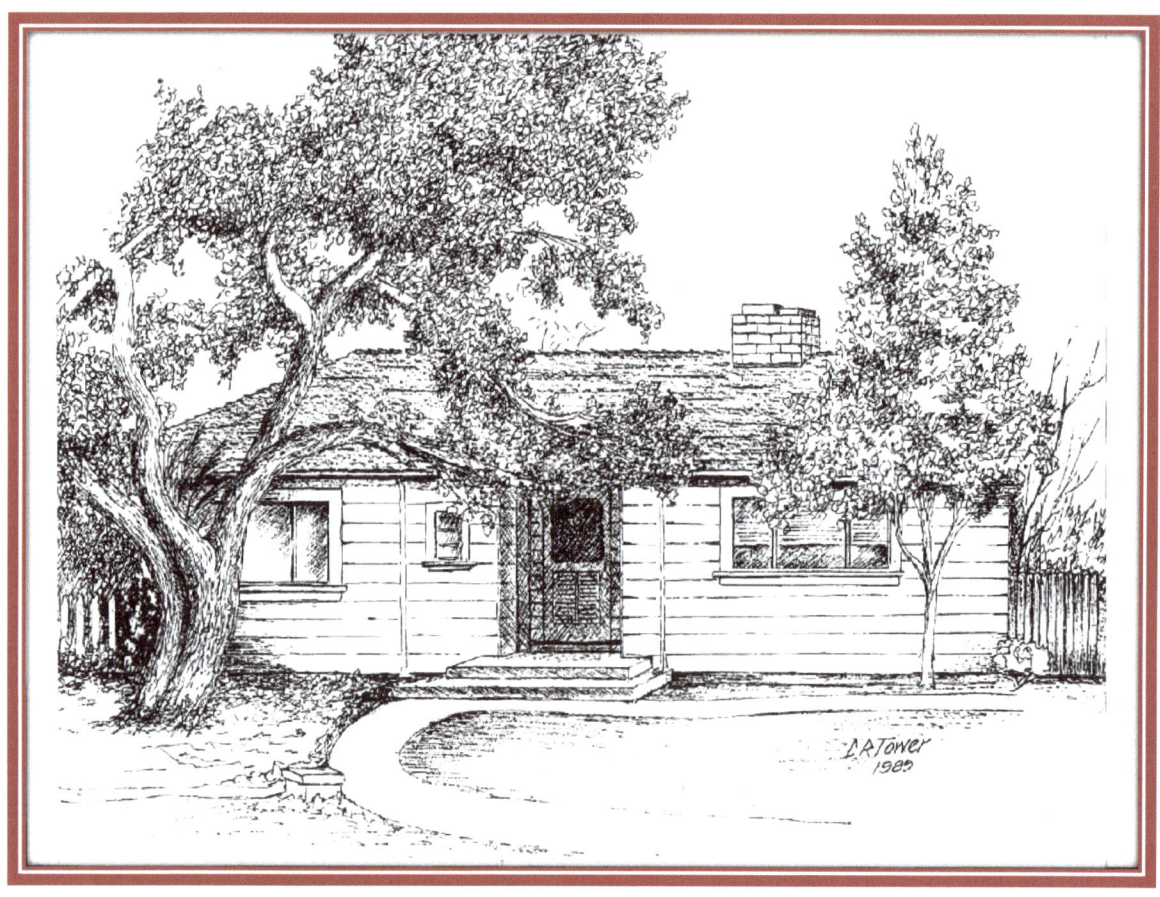

F. C. Franck, III house
1155 Washington Street

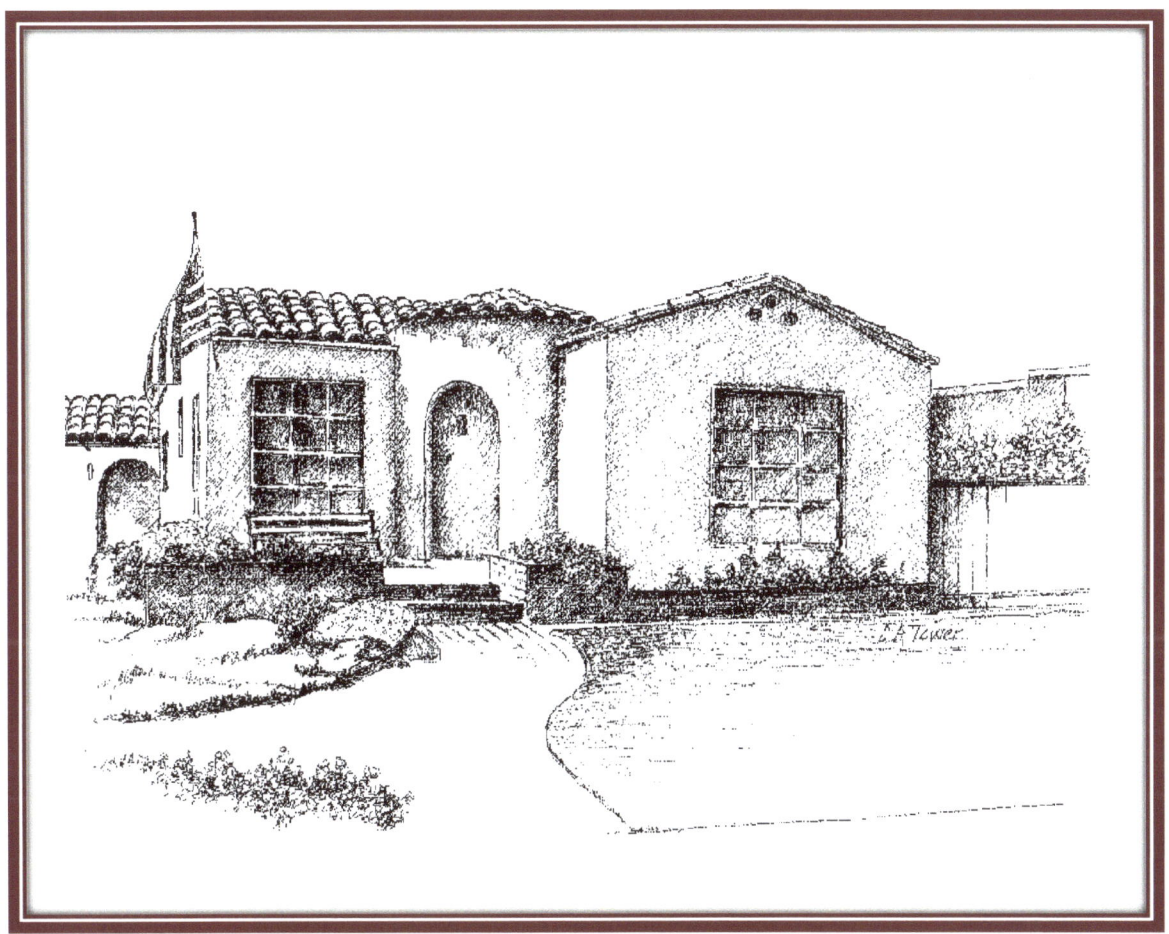

Slaven's House – 834 Main Street
(Home Tour Contributor)

City of Santa Clara Images

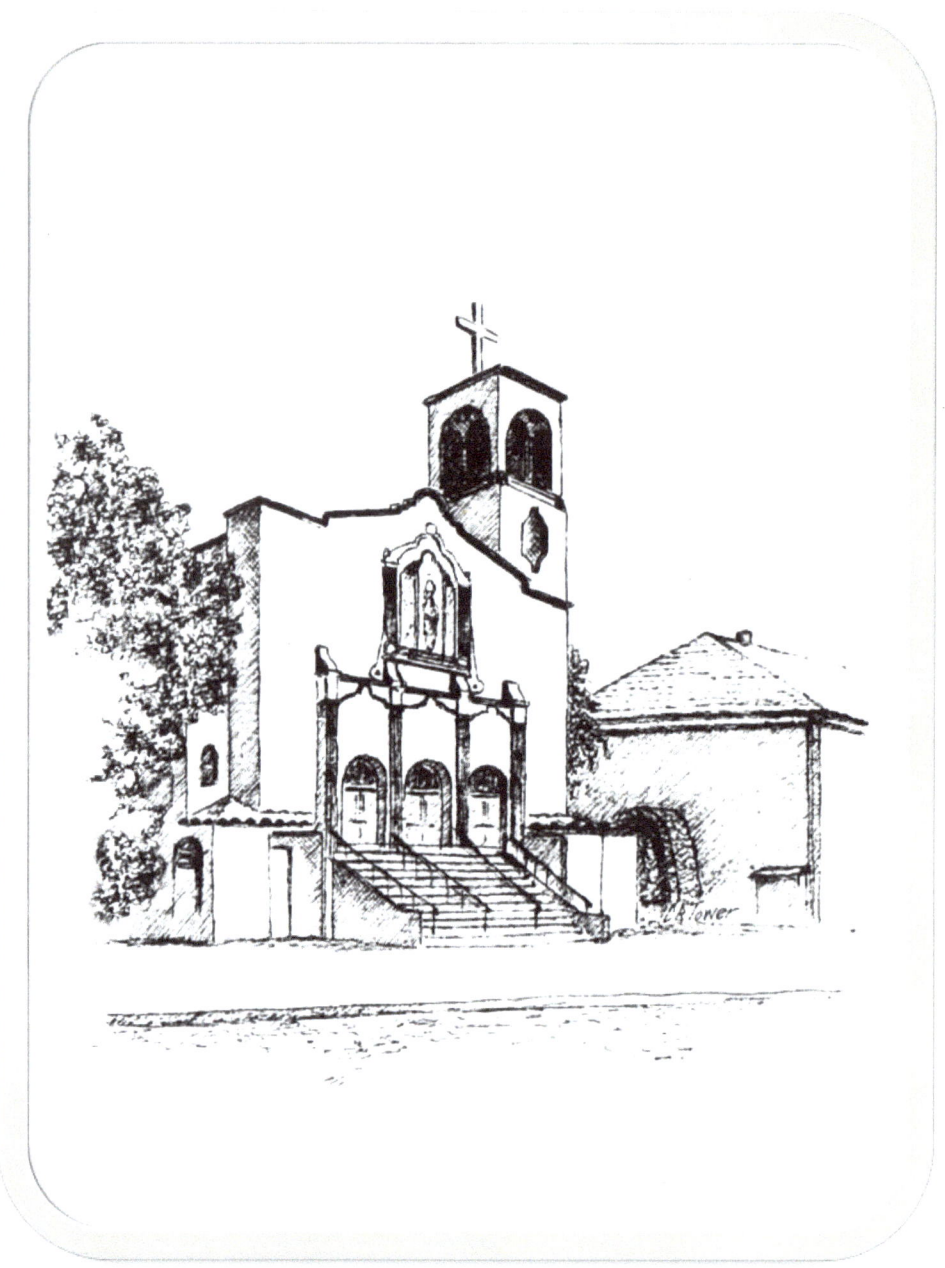

Saint Clare Church

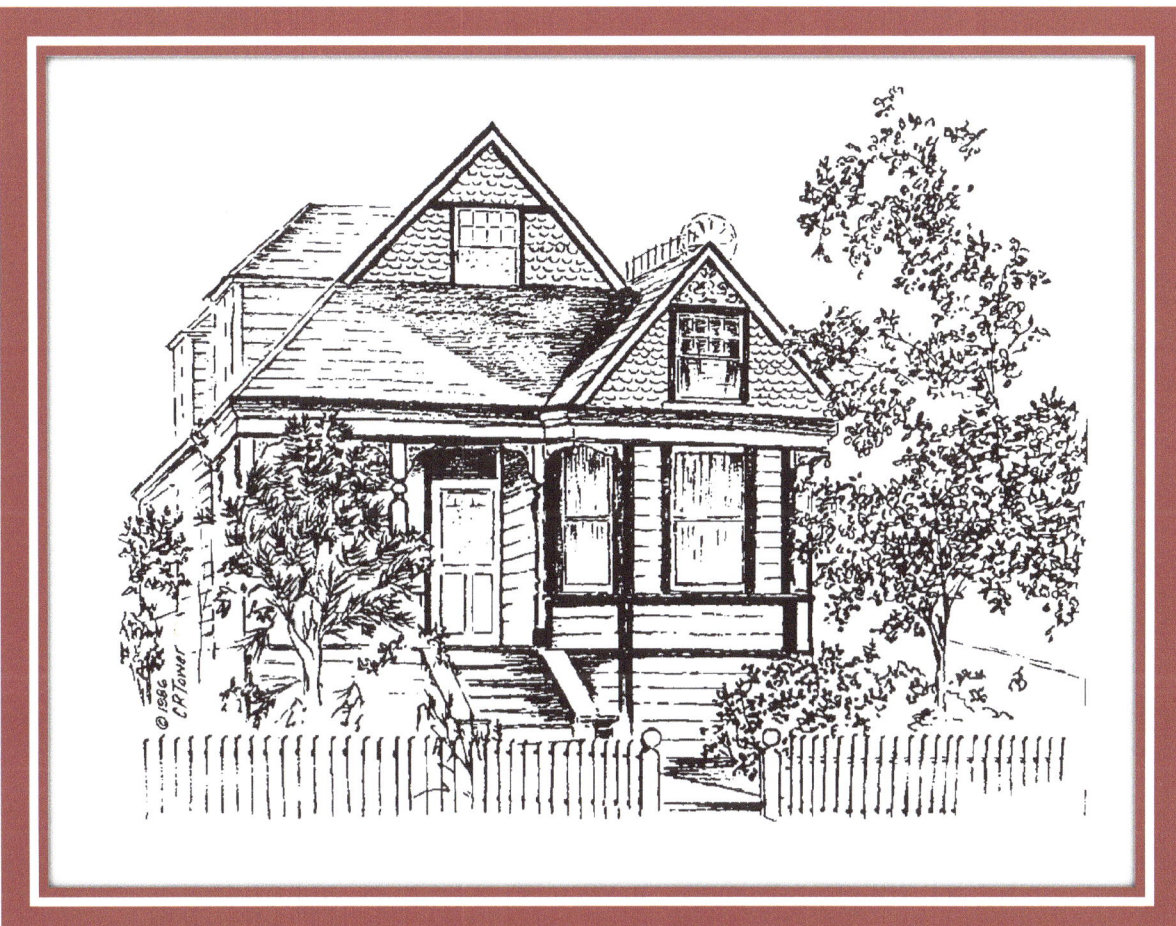

Morgan House
1390 Lincoln Street

1890s Queen Anne
1086 Madison Street

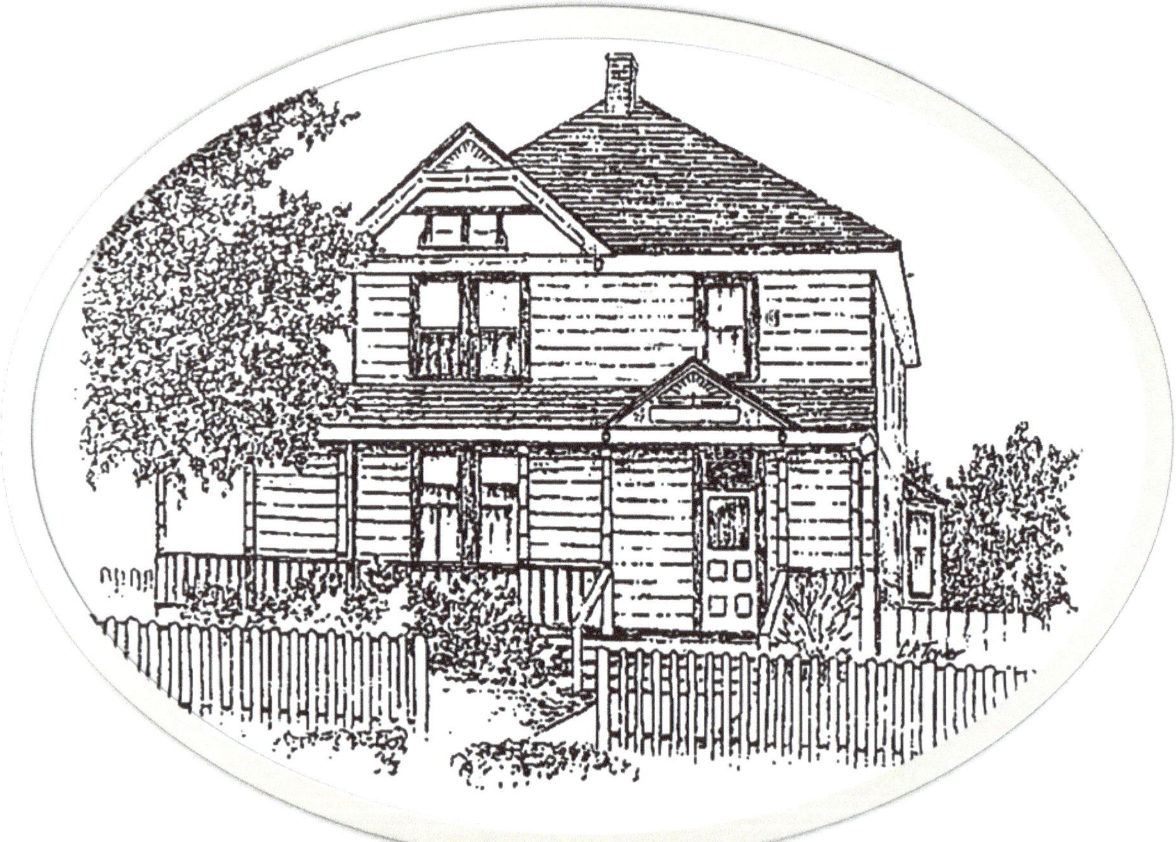

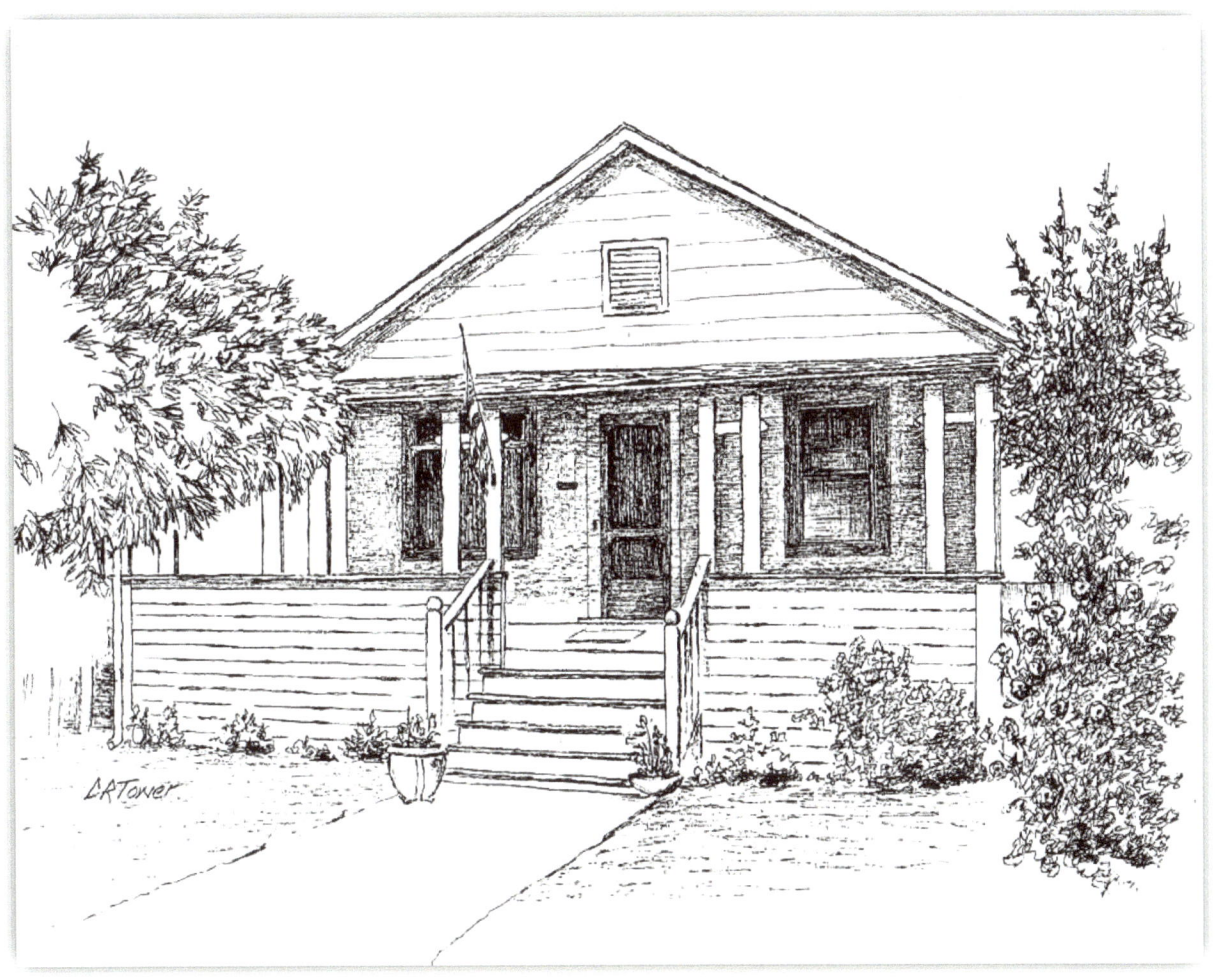

1898 Cottage
1171 Santa Clara Street

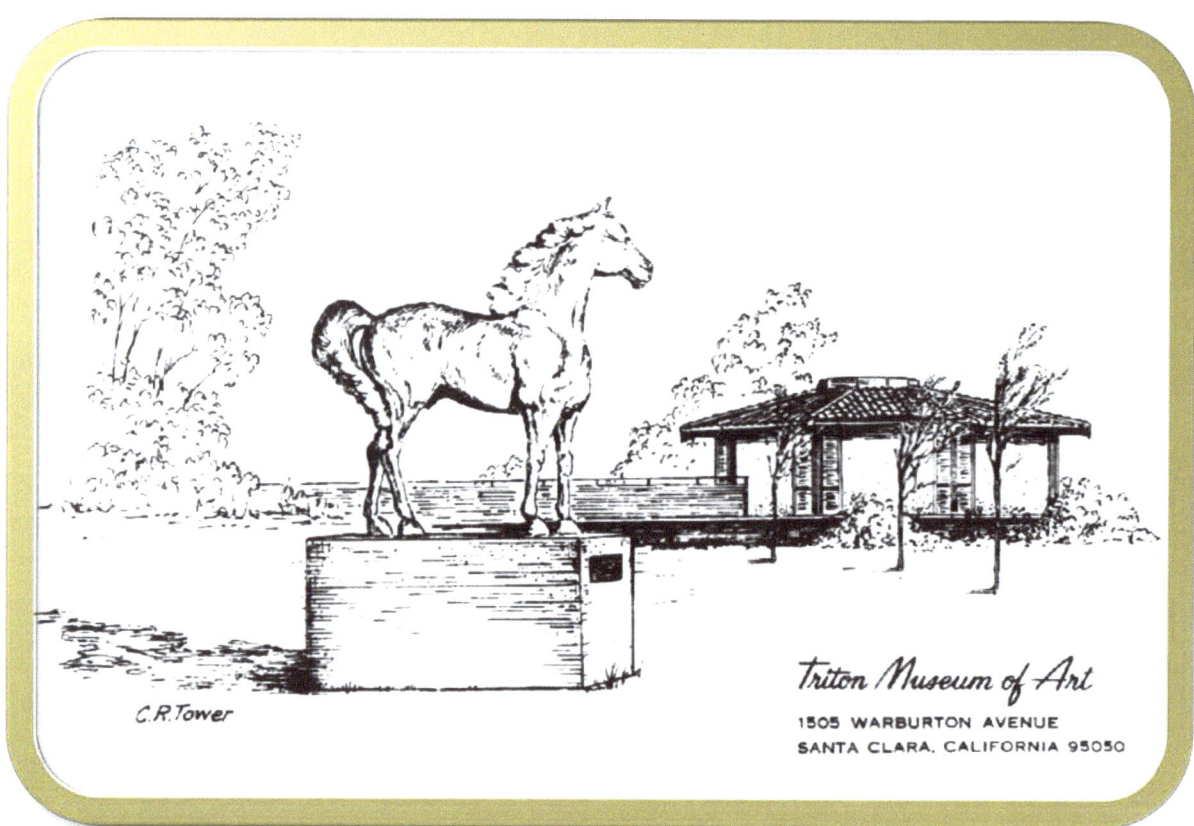

Sascha Schnittman's Morgan Horse statue on grounds of the Triton Museum of Art. The original museum consisted of an arrangement of pods similar to the one shown in the background.

The Town of Alviso – Santa Clara's neighbor at the south end of San Francisco Bay

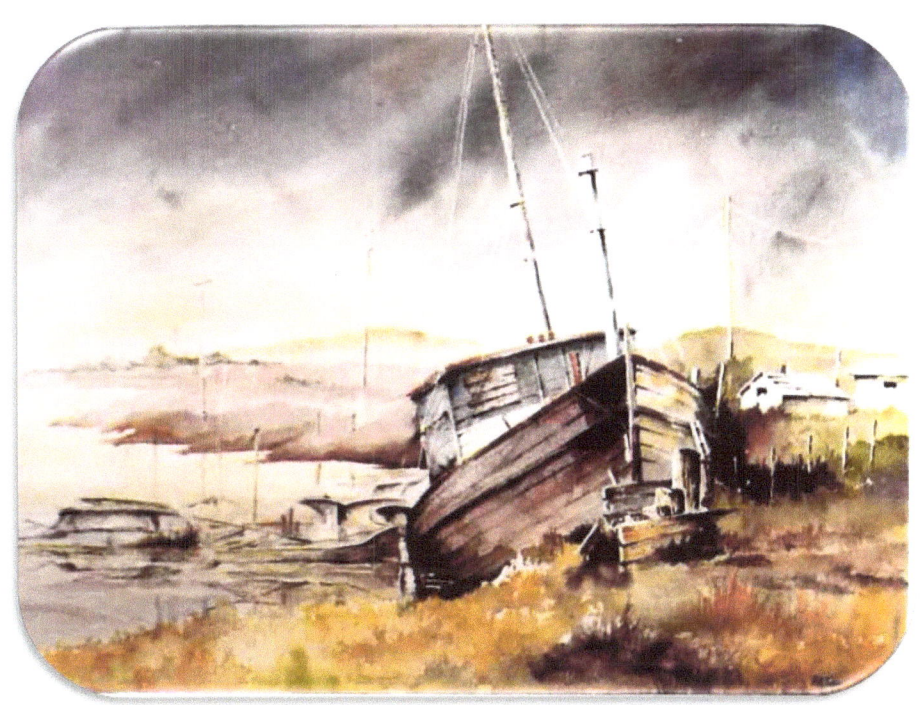

An Alviso Derelict
Alviso was once a flourishing seaport at the south end of San Francisco Bay, providing a direct connection to the City of San Francisco

More Town of Alviso

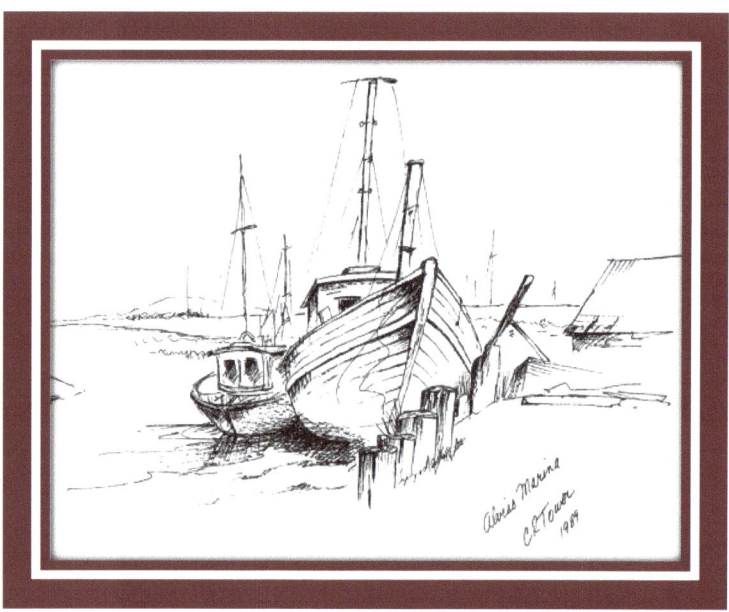

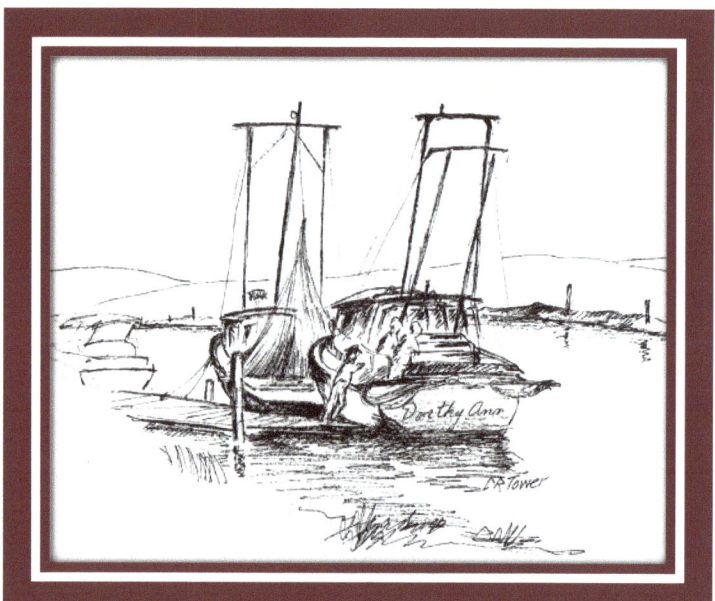

Sketching Alviso with pen and ink

Sketches of the Lost Country Life that once dominated the landscape of what is now Silicon Valley.

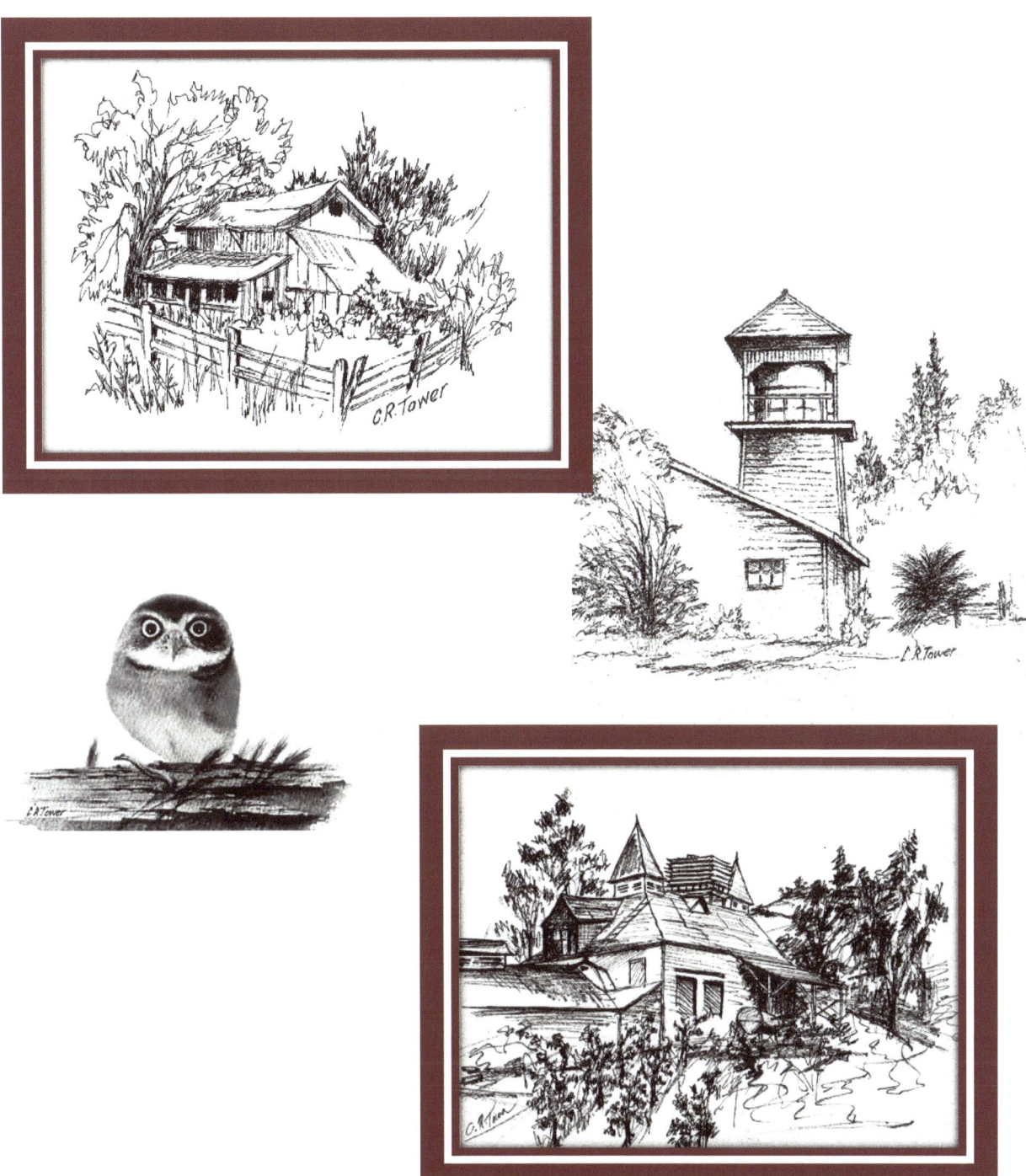

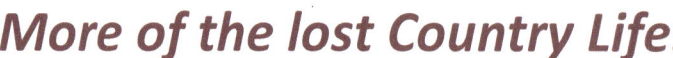

More of the lost Country Life.

(ON-SITE SKETCHES)

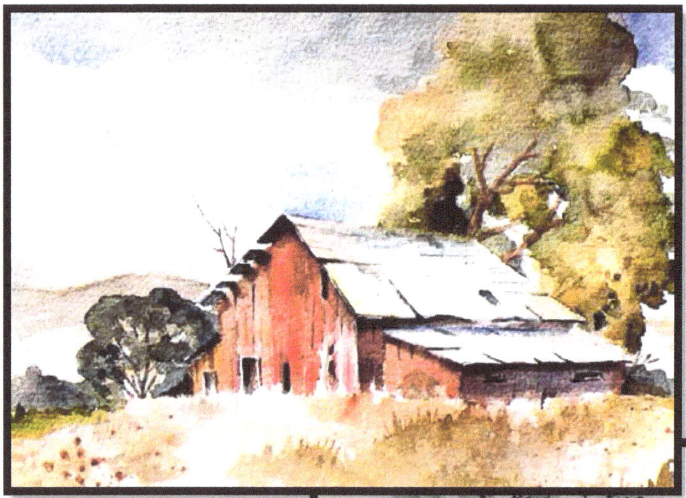

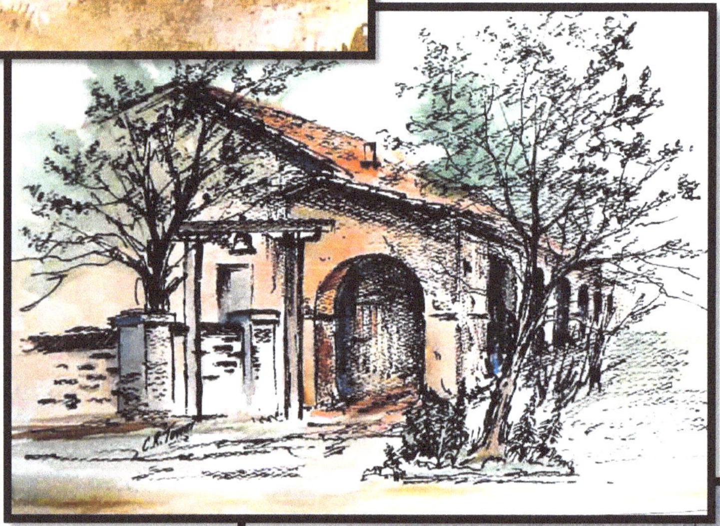

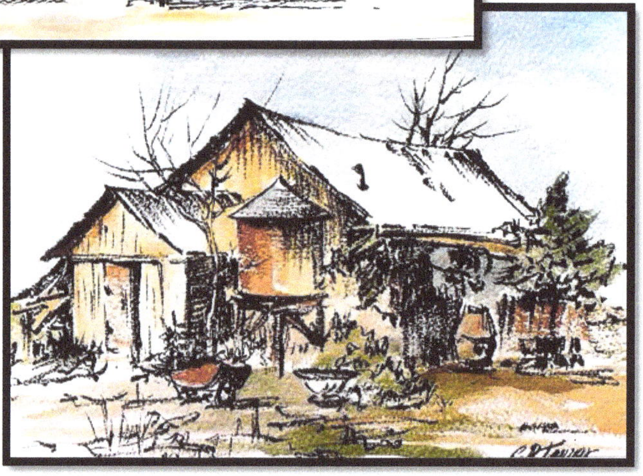

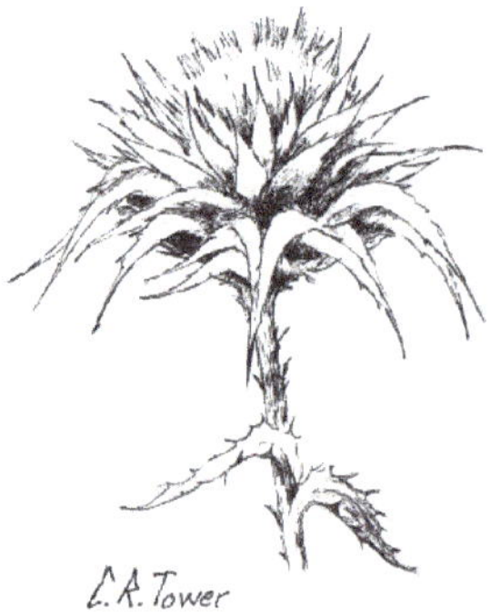

Rosicrucian Planetarium - San Jose

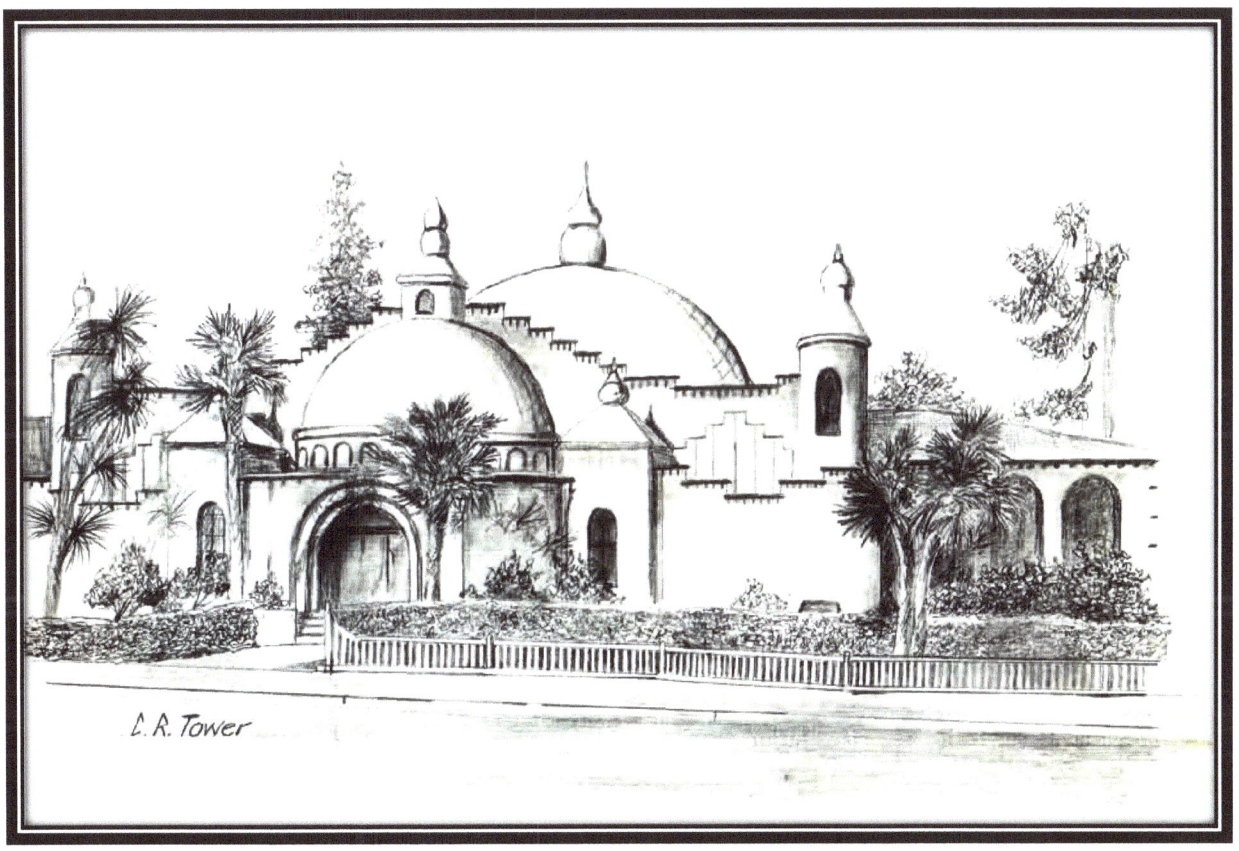

L. R. Tower

342 Naglee Avenue, San Jose
(Planetarium is on Park Avenue)
(Book Illustration)

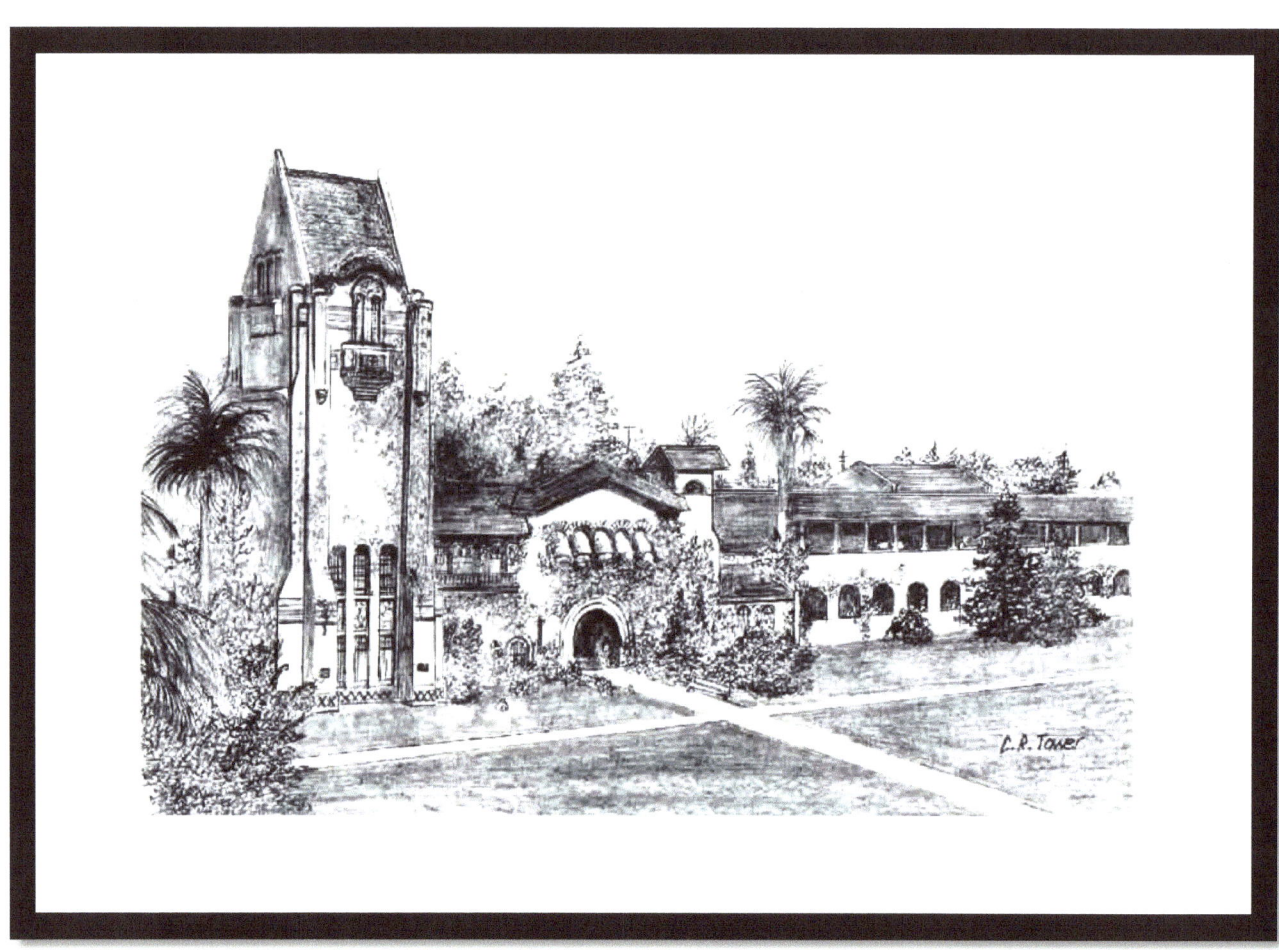

(Book Illustration)

Alum Rock Creek – San Jose

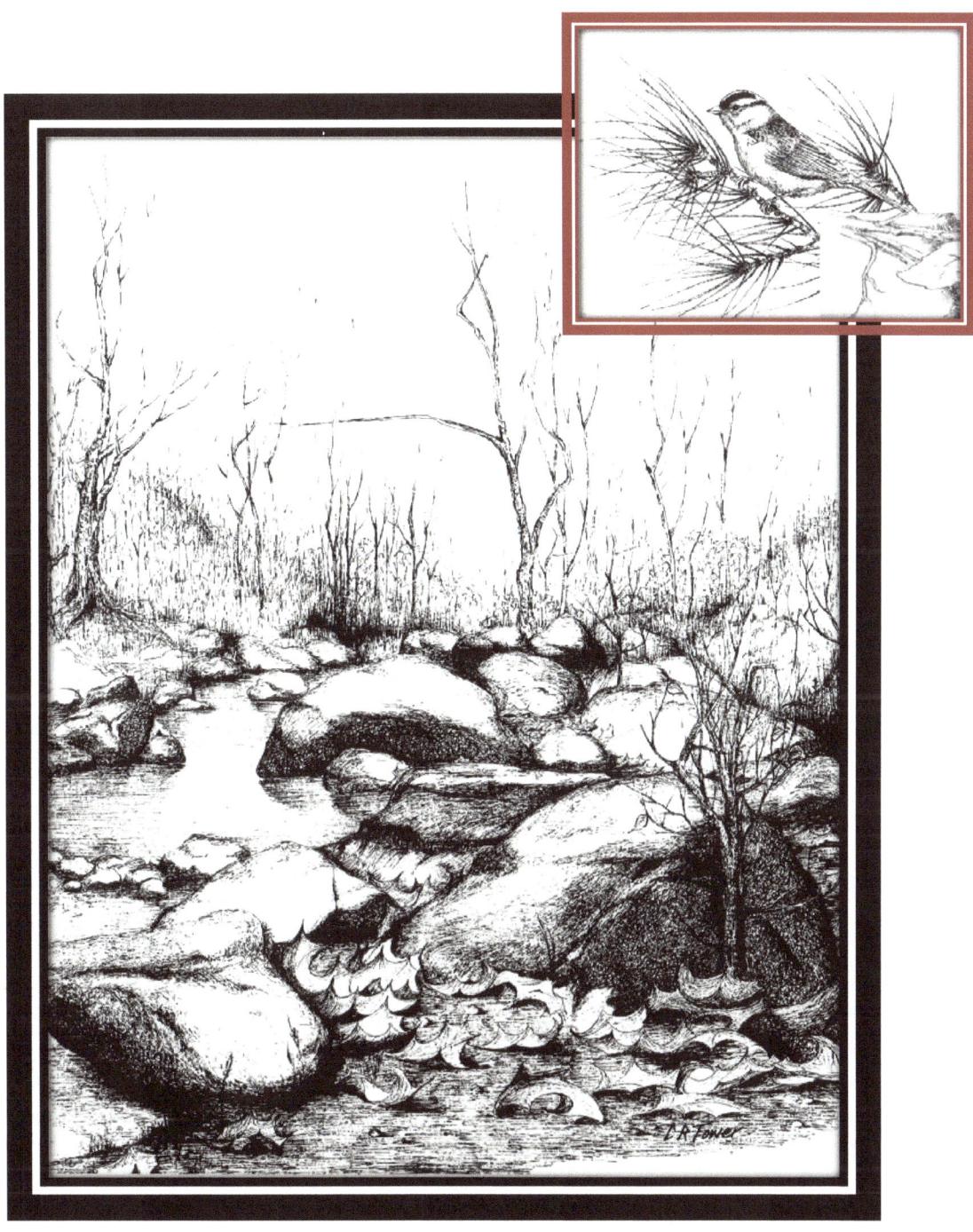

Stanford University – Palo Alto

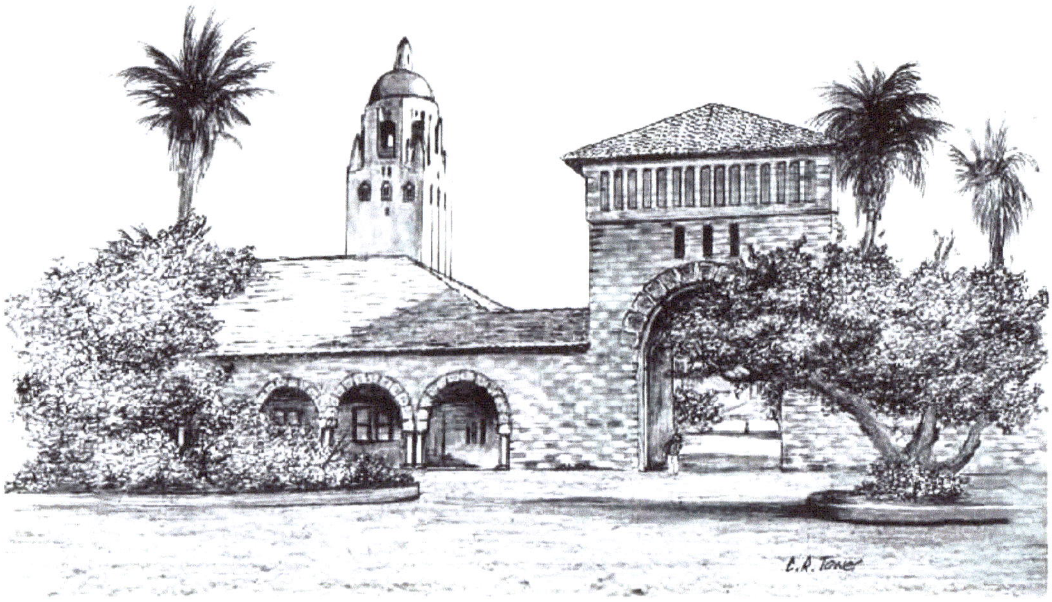

(Book Illustration)

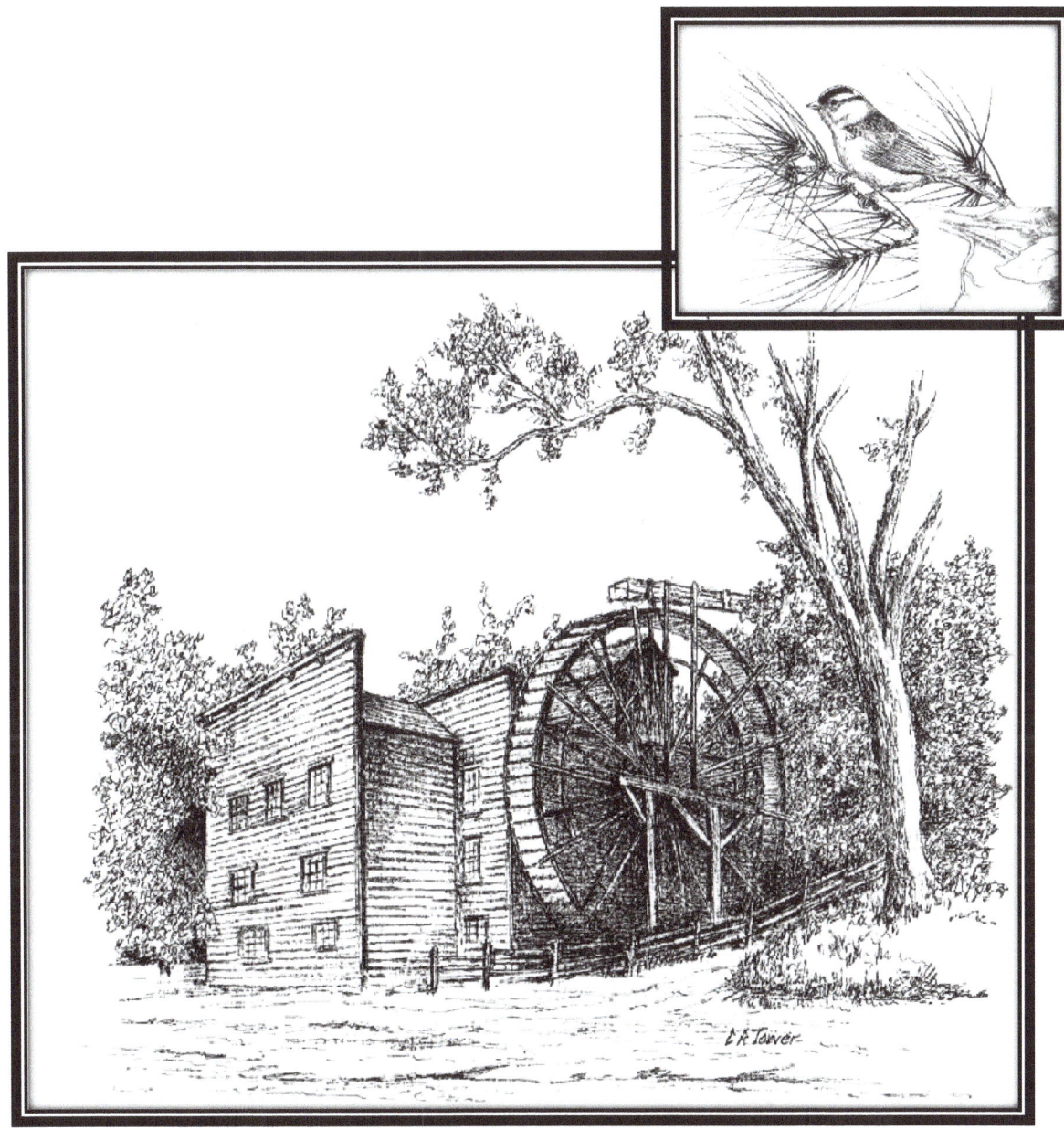

The Bale Grist Mill

Delta Resort – Bethel Island

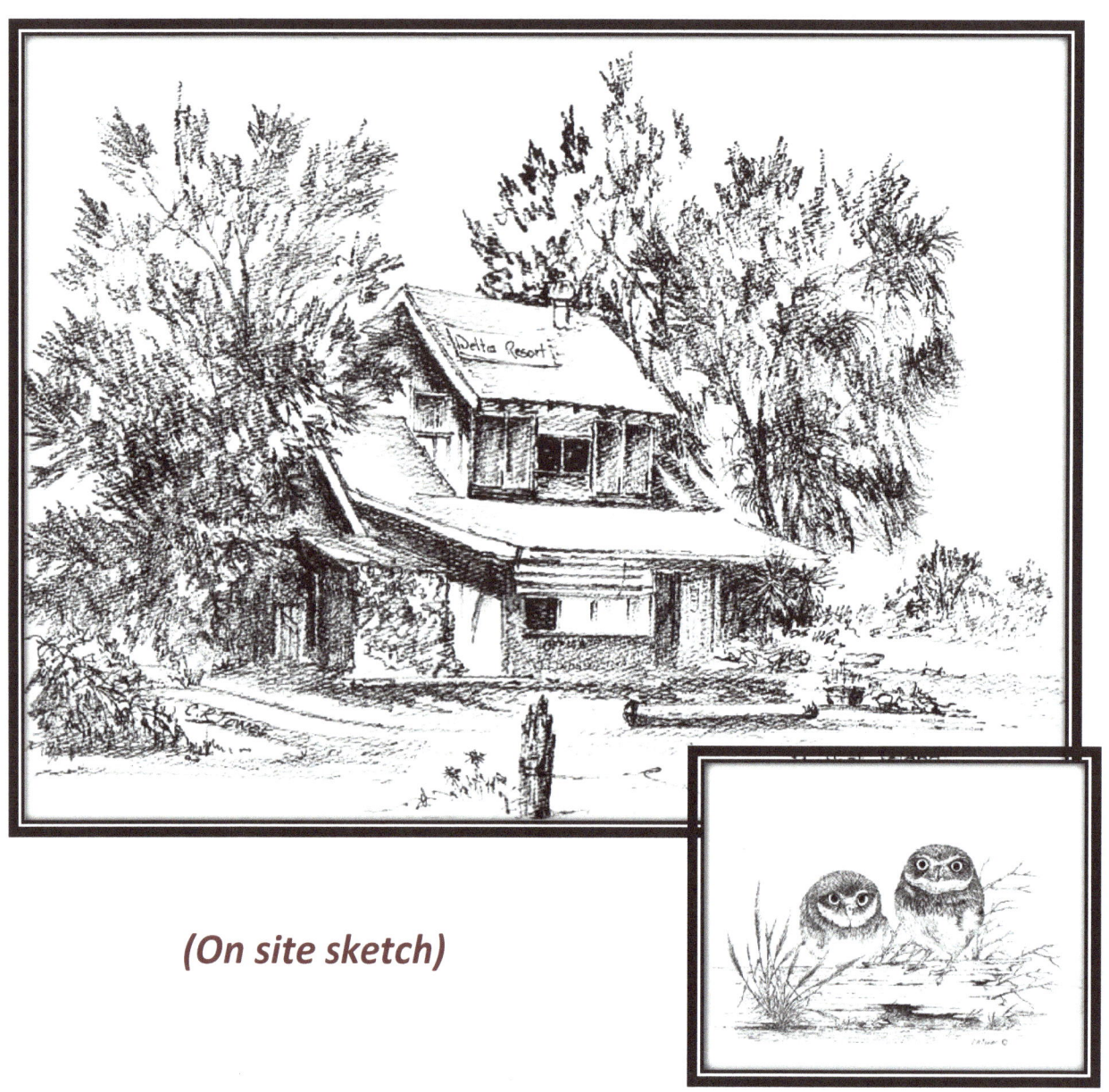

(On site sketch)

Moss Landing on Monterey Bay

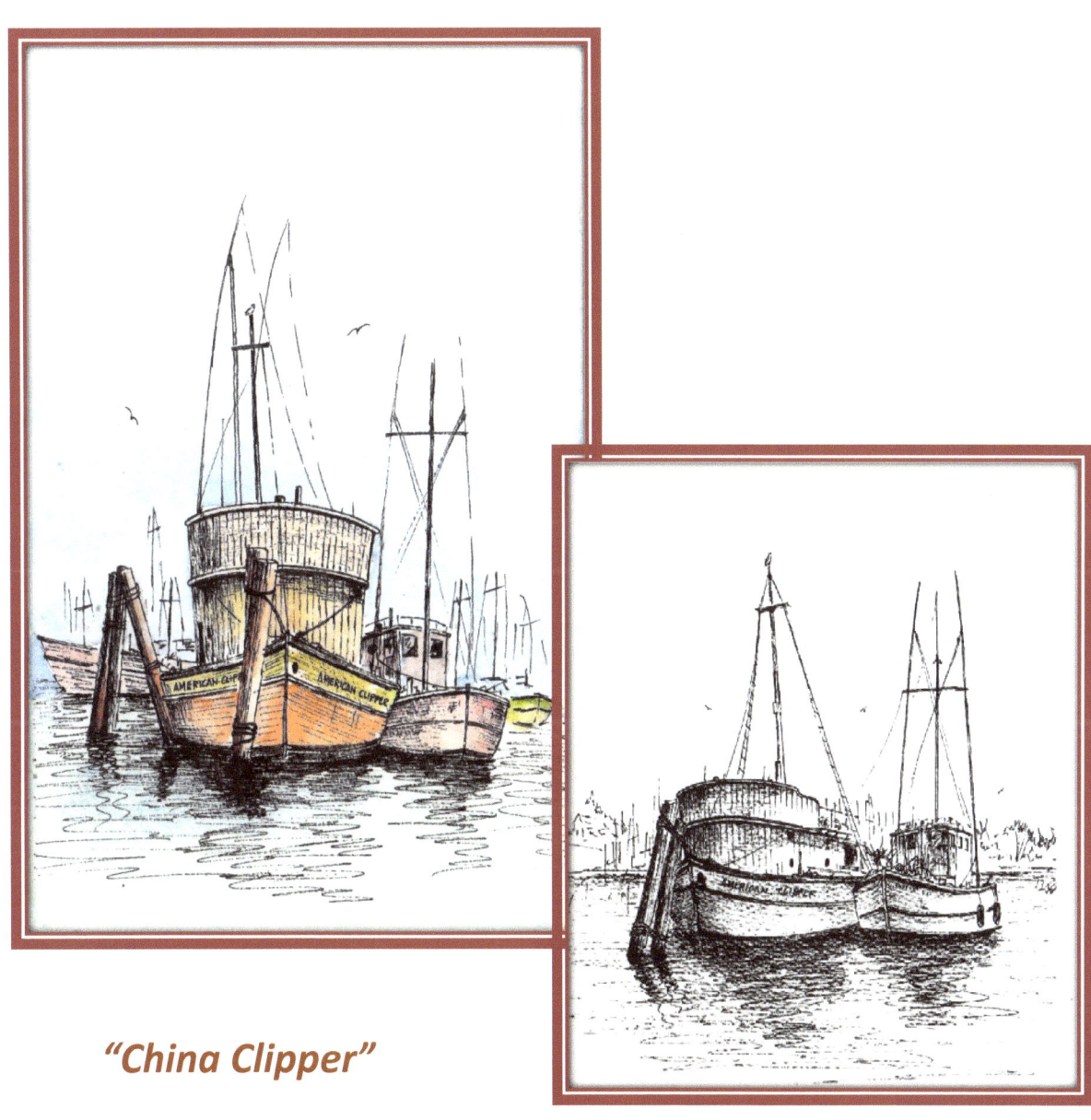

"China Clipper"

(One of my favorite subjects)

Moss Landing on Monterey Bay

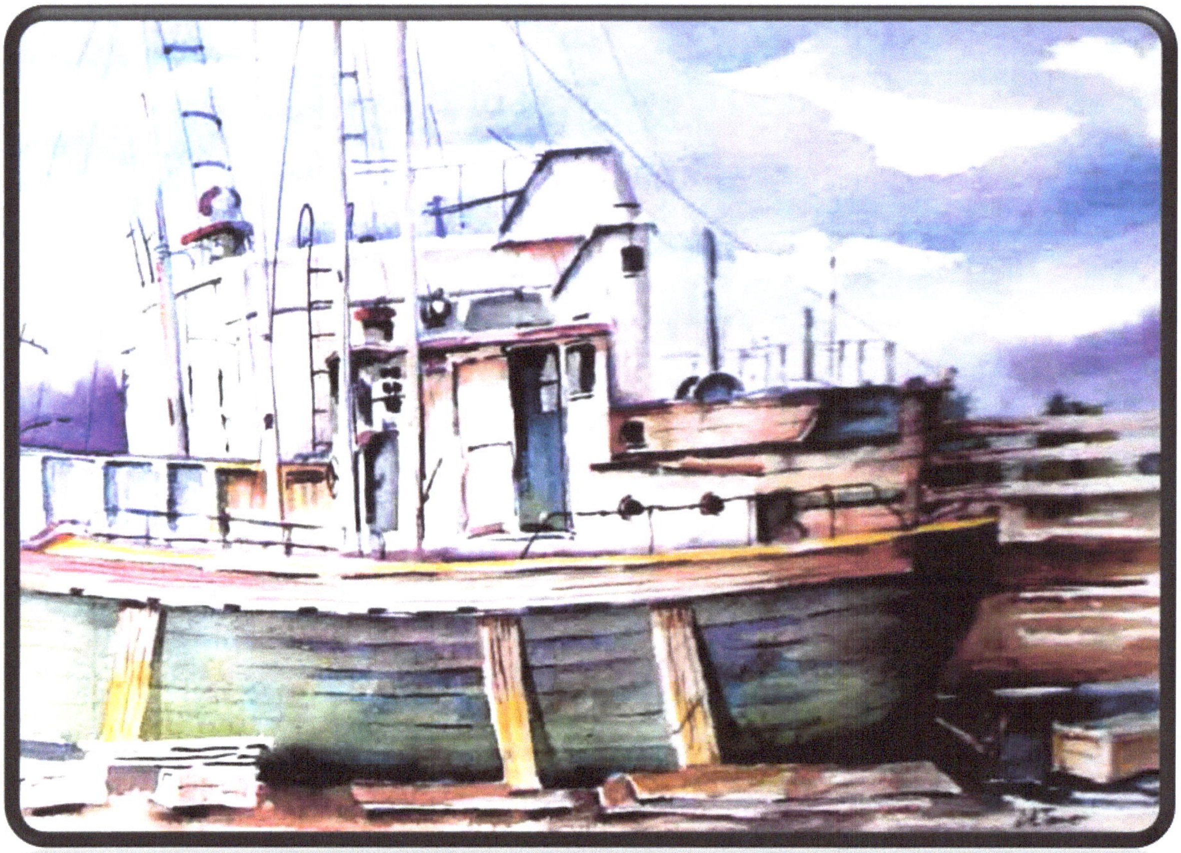

"Dry-docked – 2"
This work-in-progress could be found at the very entrance to the harbor, a short distance from California State Highway 1.

Moss Landing on Monterey Bay

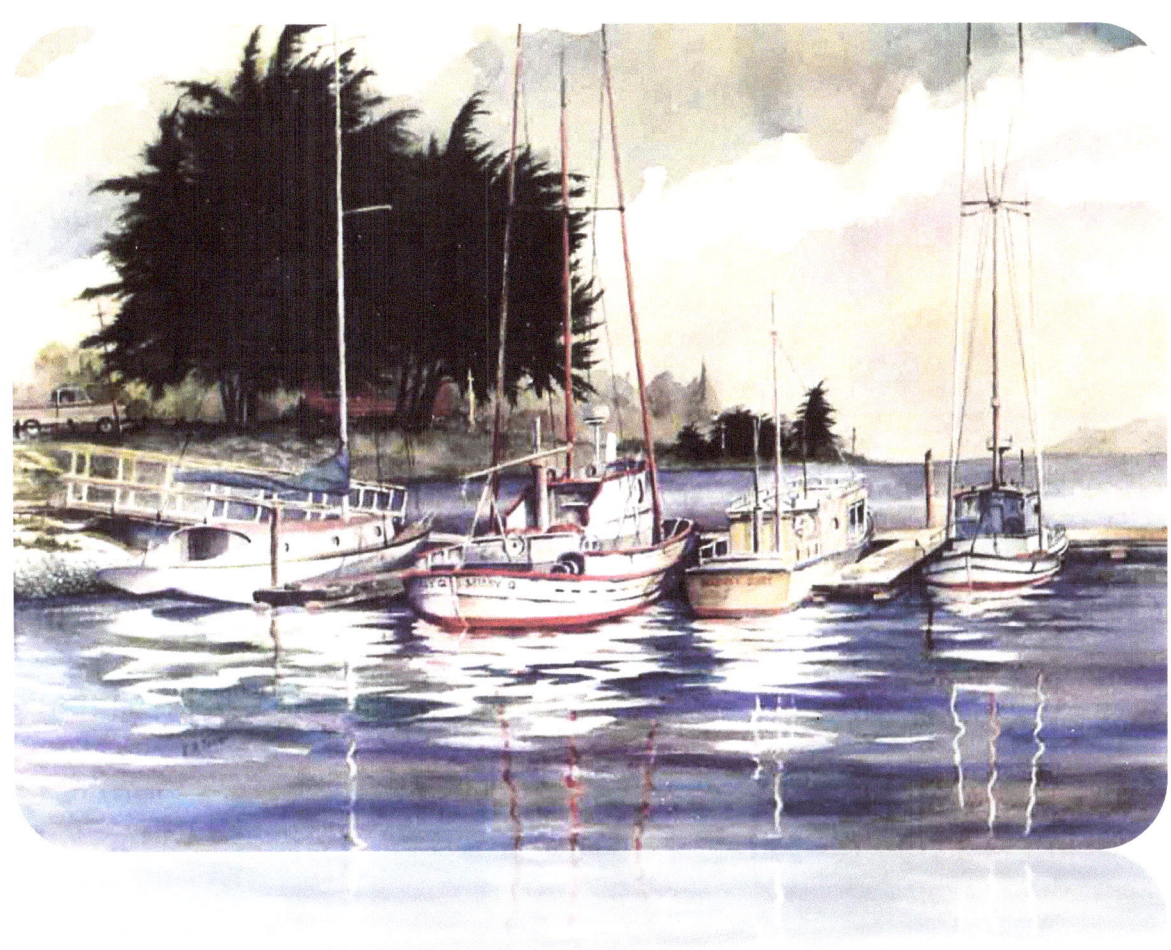

Monterey Boat Works - Monterey Bay

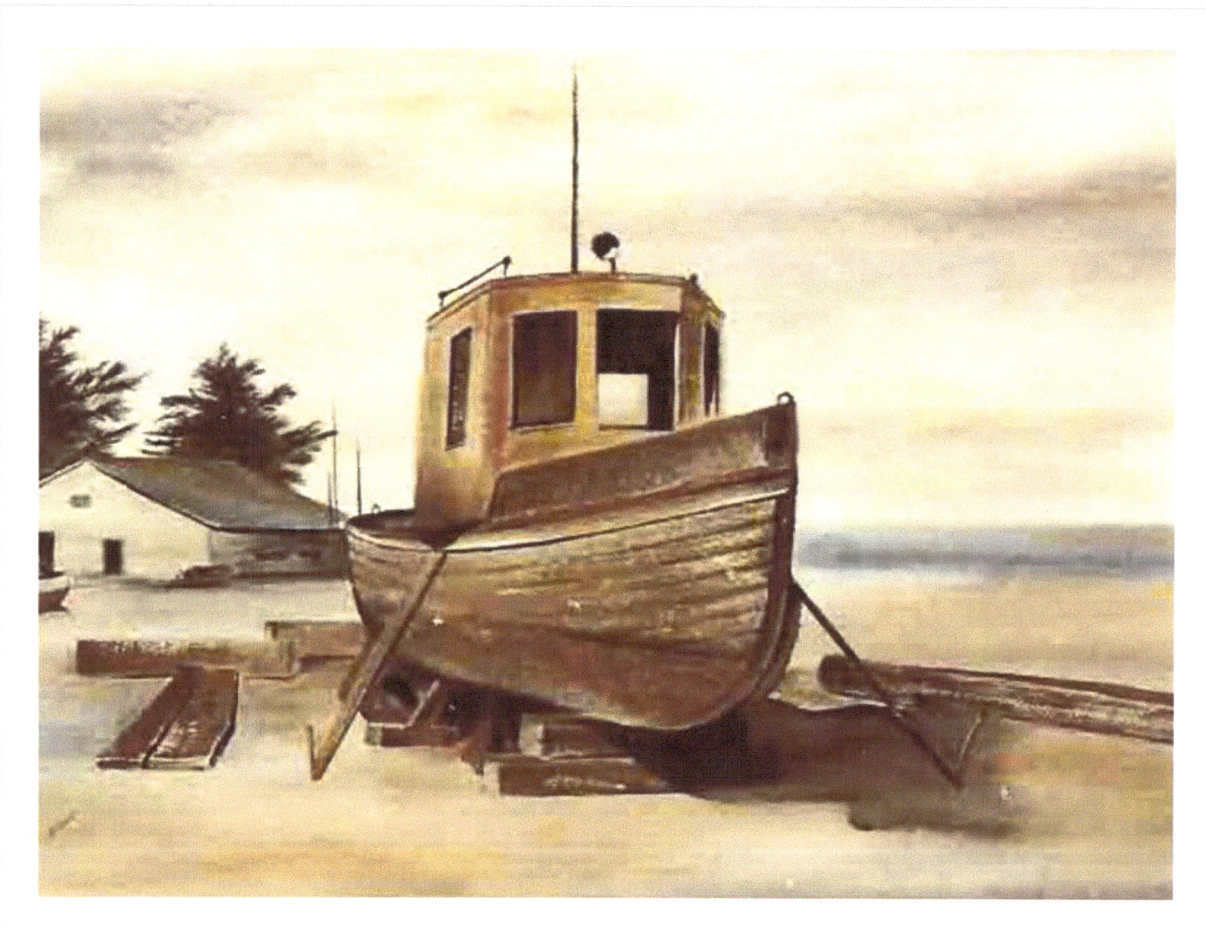

*Monterey Boat Works is located a short distance
north of the Monterey Bay Aquarium
on the road to Pacific Grove.*

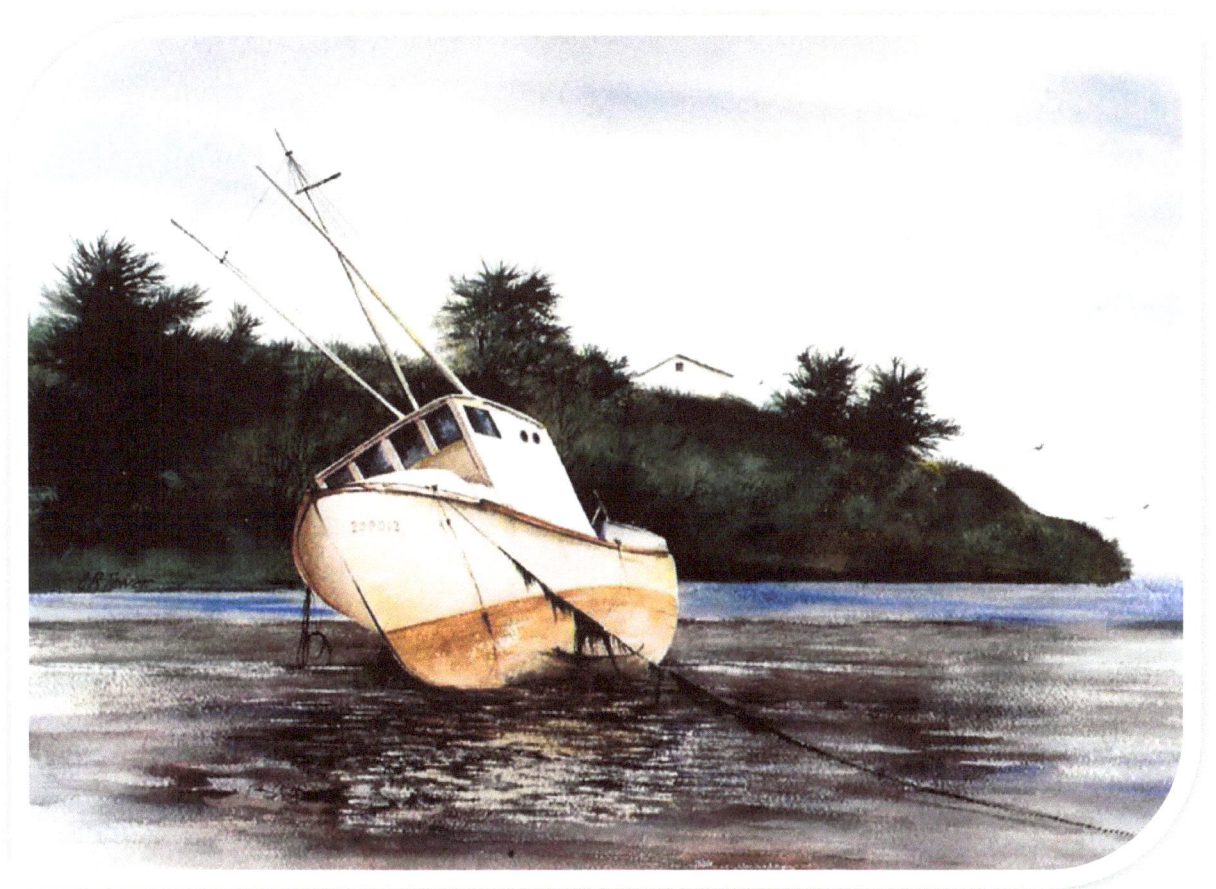

"Beached at Bodega"
Filmed at the tidelands of Bodega Bay, California
70 miles north of San Francisco - painted later.
(Movie location for Alfred Hitchcock's 1963 film "The Birds")

THE END

ABOUT THE ARTIST:

Clarence Robert Tower is a lifelong resident of California's Silicon Valley. He is self-taught artist, but can claim brief contributions to the commercial art profession with book illustrations and artistic contributions to Muscular Dystrophy national campaigns see drawing below). Mr. Tower spent his professional years as a Civil engineer and Licensed Land Surveyor during the Silicon Valley's growing years. As unusual as it might seem, his profession afforded him major contributions to his art career. Prior to the emergence of computer technology, engineering plans and Official Subdivision Maps were accomplished entirely by hand with old-style pens that were hand loaded with India ink and subsequently applied to starched linen. With that being the case, preparing these maps made up a major portion of an engineer's responsibilities. Engineering firms in those early years were somewhat judged by the artistry of their recorded documents. To keep up with competition, working engineers were compelled to become better than average artists.

After completing his published books, Seventy Years in the Silicon Valley, an Anecdotal History, The Adventures of Zack Gentry, a Tongue and Cheek History of the Opening of the West, a children's book The life of a Teddy Bear Family and an Arcadia Publications book, Legendary Locals of Santa Clara, he realized he had accumulated a huge collection of photos, digital images and image-building information, dating back 59 years, which he could pass on. Included within an assortment of pen-and-ink drawings is a significant number of Santa Clara's historical structures, many of which were visited during the city's Christmas Home Tours.

This drawing was used nationwide by Muscular Dystrophy

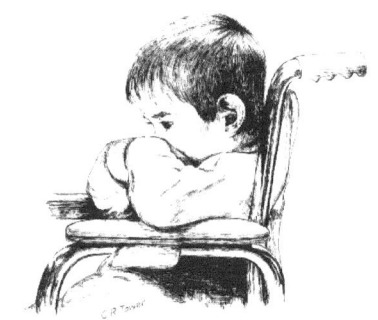